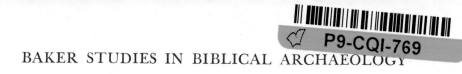
P9-CQI-769

RAS SHAMRA
AND
THE BIBLE

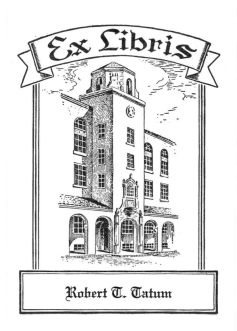

BAKER STUDIES IN BIBLICAL ARCHAEOLOGY

RAS SHAMRA AND THE BIBLE

by
Charles F. Pfeiffer

BAKER BOOK HOUSE
Grand Rapids, Michigan

Library of Congress Catalog Card Number: 62-15162

ISBN: 0-8010-7003-1

Third printing, December 1976

PHOTOLITHOPRINTED BY CUSHING - MALLOY, INC.
ANN ARBOR, MICHIGAN, UNITED STATES OF AMERICA
1976

CONTENTS

Illustrations

INTRODUCTION

Until comparatively recent times our knowledge of ancient history was restricted to the classical writings of the Graeco-Roman world. Within the past century, however, archaeologists have provided us with a body of knowledge concerning ancient cultures in Egypt, Sumer, Assyria, Babylonia, and Asia Minor. In addition to possessing thousands of artifacts discovered in these regions, we can now read documents written in cuneiform and hieroglyphic characters which date back to 3000 B.C. This material reflects a complex social structure which made use of law codes, religious and national epics, historical annals, contracts, and letters. Although little inscribed material contemporary with Old Testament history has been found in Palestine itself, discoveries made at Ras Shamra — Ugarit, along the Syrian coast, have thrown fresh light on Biblical backgrounds. Thanks to the work of careful archaeologists, Old Testament history can now be read in the light of its international context.

It is the purpose of this study to introduce the non-specialist to some of the significant discoveries made at Ras Shamra since the accidental discovery of the site in 1928. Particular attention is placed on three major epics which are named for heroes whose exploits were commemorated by the ancient inhabitants of Ras Shamra, then known as Ugarit. The poem known to us as the Aqhat Epic was earlier given the name Danel (the transliteration from Ugaritic of the name known to us as Daniel) and the Baal Epic was earlier named Anat for the sister of the god whose name it now bears. The third epic bears the name of Keret.

References to the Ugaritic epics follow the system of enumeration used by G. R. Driver in *Canaanite Myths and Legends* (Edinburgh, 1956). Transliterations and normalizations of Ugaritic names follow the same source. References to Ugaritic documents other than the epics follow Cyrus H. Gordon in his *Ugaritic Manual* (Rome, 1955).

7

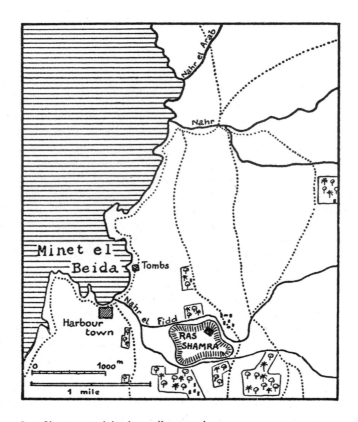

Ras Shamra and its immediate environs.

I

EXCAVATIONS AT RAS SHAMRA

In the spring of 1928 a Syrian peasant accidentally plowed up a flagstone some distance from the bay of *Minet el-Beida* ("White Harbor") on the Syrian coast. He noted that the stone covered a subterranean passage which proved to be a burial chamber. This chance event opened a whole new chapter in the history of the Near East, for it led to the excavation of a city which served as the meeting place between East and West during the middle of the second millennium B.C. Biblical studies, too, received new impetus from the important body of literature in a strange new Semitic tongue which was subsequently discovered there.

The native who came upon the burial chamber, appropriated the pottery and other objects and sold them to a local antiquities dealer. There was a time when archaeology was a matter of hunting for ancient treasure, but modern research insists that the exact place and environment of every find be noted, for only in that way can scholars determine the true significance of their discoveries. The Syrian was unaware of this fact and only thought of the immediate financial value of the articles he had found.

A report of the discovery was made to the governor of the area which was then under French rule. He notified the Bureau of Antiquities which promptly investigated the matter and sent Charles Virolleaud, a cuneiform expert, to conduct excavations at the site. The immediate results were disappointing, although pieces of Cypro-Mycenaean pottery were found in the tomb rubbish. This was the first evidence of the cosmopolitan nature of the ancient settlers of this strategic area.

Another French archaeologist, Professor René Dussaud, examined a map of the tomb and noticed its similarity to the tombs of the kings of ancient Crete. Sensing that important ruins might be found nearby he urged the *Academie des Inscriptions*

9

et Belles Lettres of the Institut de Paris to sponsor an archaeological expedition.

Less than a mile from the cemetery which the Syrian peasant had accidentally discovered is a sixty-five foot hill, overgrown with aromatic fennel which the Arabs have named *Ras Shamra* ("Fennel Head"). Subsequent discoveries identified Ras Shamra with the ancient Phoenician city of Ugarit. In the spring of 1929, a French archaeological expedition directed by F. A. Schaeffer of the Strasbourg Museum and his associate, George Chenet, began the systematic excavation of Ras Shamra. The work continued for a few months each year from 1929 to the outbreak of World War II, and it was resumed in 1950. Only a small part of the ruin has been excavated, yet it ranks as one of the most significant archeological discoveries of the twentieth century.

Excavations at Ras Shamra indicate that the site had a history extending back to the Neolithic Age — the fifth or sixth millennium B.C. Schaeffer has noted five levels of occupation which are numbered from the top down. Level five contains the flint and bone implements of the first occupants of the site, a pre-pottery Neolithic people. The fourth, or Chalcolithic level has yielded several fine examples of painted Halafian ceramics. During the course of the occupation of Level three (the latter half of the third millennium B.C.) the city was destroyed by fire. The people who subsequently occupied the site used so-called Khirbet Kerak ware.

Most of Schaeffer's work has been on the two topmost strata, numbered two (2100-1600 B.C.) and one (1600-1200 B.C.). During both of these periods Ras Shamra bore the name Ugarit. The great literary and cultural achievements of Ugarit occurred during the period represented by Level one.

THE ROYAL NECROPOLIS

The 1929 expedition met success from the very start. Native workmen found pieces of pottery dating from the second millennium B.C. almost as soon as they began digging. Nearby they came upon a necropolis with the tombs of kings who had ruled ancient Ugarit. Goblets and vases similar to those earlier discovered in Cyprus were excavated. A set of weights was found, the largest of which was equal to the Egyptian mina of 437 grams. Later there were to be many evidences of Egyptian influence at Ugarit.

A well-preserved figure of the Egyptian hawk god, Horus, covered with patina, was found at the foot of a wall. The bird

Air View of Ras Shamra. [A] indicates excavations at the northeast part of Ugarit, 1929-37; [B] indicates excavations at the northwest part of the mound, 1937. [I] shows the limits of the mound.

wears the royal crown used by the kings of Upper and Lower Egypt. Another hawk, found nearby, had plumage inlaid with gold. A uraeus, or sacred asp, customarily worn on the headdress of Egyptian Pharaohs, appears between the claws of this second hawk. Beside the two hawks the excavators found the bronze figure of a seated god who has a profile similar to that of an Eighteenth Dynasty (1570-1310 B.C.) Pharaoh. The hand of the god, raised in blessing, is not Egyptian, however.

Nearby was a well preserved figure of the Phoenician god Resheph, "the ravager." The god's right arm is raised as if to smite his foes, and his left hand holds a whip. A beautifully wrought golden mask covers his face, above which is a high, gold-plated headdress. Silver armor protects the god's body and his right arm is adorned by a golden bracelet.

Beside the statue of Resheph stood a golden image of Athtart, the Canaanite mother goddess who is known in the Old Testament as Ashtoreth and to the Greek world as Astarte. The nude goddess holds lotus flowers in her hand. Her necklace of precious stones was found near the statue.

Moving southward the excavators came upon a temple-like structure with a floor covered by large flagstones. Under this floor the kings of ancient Ugarit were buried. Their tombs, like the royal tombs of Egypt, had been rifled centuries ago. Evidently the royal ministers of Ugarit could not resist the temptation to steal the articles of silver and gold which had been reverently placed near their deceased sovereigns. Much that is of interest to the archaeologist is of little financial value, however. The tombs yielded many glass vases, alabaster and painted clay dishes, plates, and pitchers.

A gold ring decorated with an iron wire would seem incongruous to us, yet in the second millennium B.C. when tools and weapons were made of bronze, iron was a rare and precious metal. Such a ring, found in one of the royal tombs, illustrates the change in the value of precious metals.

Cylinder seals had been used among the Sumerians as early as 3000 B.C. Royal laws and decrees were "signed" by rolling a seal over a cuneiform clay tablet before it was put in the sun to harden. Such a seal turned up early in the excavation of Ugarit.

In ancient times, a robber had entered a lady's tomb, emptied her jewel case, and cast it aside. While we could wish for her jewels, the case itself has archaeological value. Its lid portrays the Cretan-Mycenaean fertility goddess on her throne. A ram, representing the male element, is on each side. Ripe ears of

Ugaritic Fertility Goddess. The cover of an ivory box found in a tomb at Ugarit depicts the popular goddess of fertility.

corn in the hands of the goddess symbolize the fruitfulness of the earth. On her head she wears a graceful Asiatic headdress. The torso is nude. From hips to feet she is covered with a much-pleated skirt with many ruffles.

The Ras Shamra Mound

Although the discoveries in the area of the royal necropolis were intensely interesting, Dr. Schaeffer also wanted to locate the ruins of the ancient port city which we now know was named Ugarit. He chose to work on the highest point of the Ras Shamra mound where a few traces of wall were visible among the shrubs. Again success was instantaneous. The foundations of a large building were discovered with ashes between the walls affording evidence that it had been destroyed by fire. A bronze dagger and nail found among the ruins dated from the same

Jars from the Harbor Town. More than 80
jars for oil or wine were discovered at one spot,
evidently an ancient store.

Ceremonial Adzehead. The
adzehead bears an inscription
in the Ugaritic cuneiform alphabet.

Funeral Vault. Under the courtyard or the rooms of the ground
floor each house at Ugarit had
a funeral vault in which deceased members of the family
were buried.

period as the royal necropolis. A life size statue of an Egyptian Pharaoh from the time of Tutankhamon (ca. 1353-1344 B.C.) was discovered between the caved-in walls of the building. Tables inscribed with hieroglyphs afforded evidence that the kings of Ugarit were friends and allies of the Egyptians.

THE LIBRARY

The most significant find of the entire expedition was a room containing a large number of clay tablets written in cuneiform characters. Some were in Akkadian, the Semitic tongue spoken by the ancient Babylonians and Assyrians which was the *lingua franca* of the Near East during the Amarna Age — the fifteenth and fourteenth centuries B.C. Others were written in Sumerian, Hurrian, Egyptian, Hieroglyphic Hittite, Cuneiform Hittite, and the language of a Cypro-Minoan linear script. Most of the tablets, however, were written in a previously unknown alphabetic script which dates back to the same Amarna period. The decipherment of this alphabet and the study of the new language used in the texts were to occupy Semitic scholars for many years. The "new" Semitic language became known as Ugaritic. The documents, later to be augmented by new discoveries, provided important information on the history and customs of ancient Syria, the nature of Canaanite religion, and the meaning of Biblical vocabulary and idiom which became meaningful in the light of Ugaritic usage. The newly discovered alphabetic script provided material for the study of the origins of alphabetic writing.

The room in which the texts were found appears to have served as a library. It was situated in a building located between the two great temples of ancient Ugarit — one dedicated to Baal and the other to Dagan.

The first expedition at Ras Shamra was ended after the discovery of a pile of seventy-four bronze weapons and tools at the foot of a cellar stairway. A number of the most beautiful of the weapons contained inscriptions in the cuneiform alphabet which had been used on the clay tablets.

SUBSEQUENT EXPEDITIONS

The initial work of Schaeffer at Ras Shamra had been amazingly successful. More money was needed if the work was to continue, and this was generously provided by the *Academie des Inscriptions* in Paris, the Louvre, and the French Department of

Public Education. As a result of this joint effort the successes of the first expedition were multiplied in succeeding years.

A large building with thirty rooms and corridors was found in the necropolis area. The building was connected by a tunnel to the tombs of the kings. It was evidently designed to provide the deceased monarchs all the blessings in the future life which they had enjoyed while reigning in Ugarit. In the dirt beneath the rooms many articles were found — bronze tools, gold and silver brooches, and many idols associated with the Canaanite fertility cult.

Stone altars were discovered in the chapels of the dead kings. These were surrounded by votive vases of painted ceramic and often adorned with reliefs. Frescoes in Egyptian tombs from the time of Tutankhamon mention such vases as gifts sent to the Pharaohs by kings of Crete and Syria.

The tomb of a royal princess yielded one thousand clay vases and hundreds of small, delicately made perfume bottles, with cups, jugs, plates, and two-handled jars in abundance. More than two hundred of these articles were in perfect condition after having been buried in the earth for thirty-five hundred years. Perhaps the most artistic pieces to be found in the princess' tomb were the seven carved ivory vases which formed part of a white alabaster toilet set. The vases are in the form of a duck resting on the water, with the head gracefully turned backward and the wings serving as a cover. Egyptian and Syrian ivory work such as that found at Ugarit has been discovered elsewhere containing red, blue, and yellow cosmetic paint. On the floor of the princess' chamber the excavators found necklaces of varicolored glass, carnelian, and other kinds of beads. Golden plates containing chiseled images of Athirat (Astarte) served as breast ornaments for the princess.

Schaeffer and his associates also engaged in further excavation at the mound, or city hill of Ugarit. They discovered a large temple located in a vast rectangular courtyard surrounded by strong walls. Large stone basins in the sanctuary were probably used for ritual bathing. Images of the gods worshiped in this temple were destroyed by vandals thirty-five hundred years ago, but modern archaeologists patiently fitted the pieces together. The result was a restored fertility goddess and a life size god resembling the figures of ancient Egyptian deities. The temple was a shrine to the god of Dagan. Costly weapons of bronze and hunting implements were found nearby.

Pieces of a great sphinx made of green stone were found in the south courtyard of the sanctuary, near a broad monumental staircase. On the breast of the sphinx was the hieroglyphic inscription of Amenemhet III (*ca.* 1835-1785 B.C.). A dedicatory inscription on the sphinx stated that the Pharaoh had given it to the god of the Ras Shamra temple. Nearby was the sculptured portrait of Chnoumit, "of the beautiful crown," the wife of Senwosret II (*ca.* 1906-1888 B.C.) Chnoumit is thought to have been a Syrian.

Further evidence of the relations between the Egyptian Pharaohs and the city states of Syria and Palestine during the fifteenth and fourteenth centuries, B.C., has been preserved in the Amarna tablets, discovered in Egypt in 1887. These letters make it clear that Egyptian rulers liked to have Syrian princesses in their harems. Marriages were useful means of cementing friendships and forming political alliances. The presence of a Syrian bride in the Egyptian court would serve as a guarantee of cordial relations between the two countries.

Although foreign wives often rose to great power in the court of Egypt they did not lose contact with the religion of their native lands. When the child of a Syrian queen became sick in Egypt, she would ask that a favorite temple goddess be sent to effect a cure. If the child regained its health, a gift would be presented to the temple which had provided the idol.

Native Syrian craftsmen frequently copied the style of imported materials and it is not always easy to distinguish the original from the copy. Broken pieces of a white limestone sphinx were discovered near the Egyptian sphinx of Amenemhet III but its rough workmanship has caused some scholars to suggest that it is of Syrian rather than Egyptian origin.

Near the temple, excavators came upon the image of a snake priestess with a large snake coiled about her breast and hips. The priestess was holding the neck of the serpent in her hands. The snake was a favorite object of worship in ancient Crete, Syria, and Palestine. Many small silver snakes similar to those offered as sacrifices by worshipers were found around the Ras Shamra sanctuary.

A large statue of the Syrian god Teshub was discovered outside the west wall of the temple where the land slopes sharply toward the lower city. Teshub holds a lance in his left hand. He has a high crown on his head, a narrow kilt around his hips, and a scepter in his right hand. The sandals on his feet have pointed toes which are of Hittite origin.

A second sanctuary, dedicated to Baal, was found west of the great Dagan temple. The large vase discovered there contained a pair of gods made of solid silver overlaid with gold. These were probably the gift of a wealthy donor to the temple.

Not far away the excavators came upon a huge stele which weighed more than a ton. On one side it contained a bas relief of the god Baal (Hadad) holding a lance in his left hand. From its wooden shaft sprang small twigs representing a fruit-bearing tree.

Further excavations have been conducted in the area where the first written materials were discovered. Schaeffer and his associates identified the structure as a library and a school for scribes who were taught by priests of the nearby Baal temple. One of the teachers, Rabana, son of Sumejana, called himself "a submissive slave of the goddess Nisaba." He carefully completed a dictionary on clay and wrote his name in the margin as author. Many practice tablets used by the students have been found. Cross lines, drawn for aid in writing; the repetition of words; and the uncertain hand of the neophyte betray the origin of these tablets.

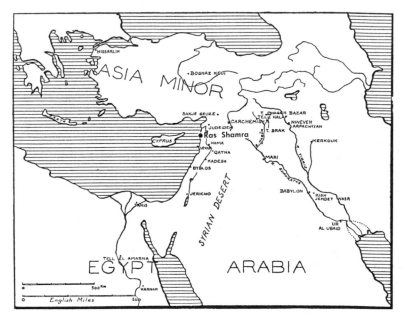

Ras Shamra (ancient Ugarit) and its ancient neighbors.

II

UGARIT IN HISTORY

The bay known as Minet el-Beida is located just fifty nautical miles opposite the point of the island of Cyprus. The ancient Greeks named it *Leucos Limen*, "white harbor," because of the glaring calcareous rocks which protect the harbor entrance. A port town located nearby at the Ras Shamra mound is known to have been occupied as early as the fifth millennium B.C. Sargon of Akkad (*ca.* 2360 B.C.) may have passed through Ras Shamra, for his inscriptions boast that he reached the Mediterranean. Rulers of the Third Dynasty of Ur (*ca.* 2060-1950 B.C.) also appear to have had contact with Ras Shamra. Pottery discovered among its ruins has definite Mesopotamian influence.

Between 2400 and 2300 B.C. the city was burned and its older population was displaced. Amorites and Semitic Canaanites migrated northward and the Canaanite people known to us as Phoenicians settled along the Mediterranean coast of northern Syria. The Phoenicians controlled Cyprus at this period and Cypriote pottery is identical in design with that found at Ras Shamra.

STRATEGIC LOCATION

In subsequent years Ras Shamra, or Ugarit as it was then called, became the channel through which Mediterranean culture penetrated Western Asia. The "White Harbor" was particularly important during the Bronze Age when ships from Cyprus laden with copper ore stopped there to unload cargo destined for Mesopotamia. At that time it served as the crossroads between the cultures of the Mediterranean region and the Sumero-Akkadian world.

Products of the Mediterranean and the Red Sea were brought to the port city of Ugarit. Gold, incense, perfumes, and even exotic animals were exchanged there for wood, leather, and

19

weapons and utensils made of bronze. By the early years of the second millennium B.C., Ugarit had become the great trading center between Mesopotamia and Egypt. Pharaohs of the Twelfth Dynasty (*ca.* 1991-1786 B.C.) used its facilities for trade with the Babylonian Empire. The name Ugarit which appears in the literature of Tell el-Amarna, Mari, and Bogaskoy, first appears at the beginning of the second millennium as the name of the city located at Ras Shamra.

ALLIANCE WITH EGYPT

Following the death of Hammurabi of Babylon (*ca.* 1686 B.C.), the Tigris-Euphrates area experienced a period of disorder. Kassite invaders from the Zagros Mountains brought about the fall of the Babylonian dynasty. Internal troubles developed at Ugarit and the aggressive policies of the Hittite Empire centered in Asia Minor threatened the whole of northern Syria. With warlike tribes ruling Mesopotamia, Ugarit found it wise to cultivate friendly relations with Egypt as a means of security against foreign encroachments. Among the discoveries at Ugarit is a stela which notes an offering for the soul of Senwesret-Ankh, an Egyptian official who may have been an ambassador to Ugarit.

Egypt, too, found it politically expedient to cultivate friendly relations with Syria. By making alliances with the petty kings of Palestine and Syria, Egypt protected her frontiers and guaranteed supplies of wood and other raw materials.

The alliance between Egypt and Ugarit did not hinder Ugarit's commercial relations with the Aegean world. Cretan culture reached a high point by the nineteenth century B.C. and Cretan products were much appreciated in Ugarit. A cup discovered in one of the Ras Shamra tombs in 1936 was identified by Sir Arthur Evans as identical in design with those found in the palace at Knossos.

The influx of Aegeans from Crete and their settlement along the Syrian coastal regions is echoed in both Greek and Ugaritic literature. Greek legends speak of a King Kasios who came to the region of Ugarit with Achaeans and Cretans during the second millennium B.C. Mount Cassius is probably named for this king. The Ugaritic epic of Keret is thought to reflect the name of Crete.

THE HURRIANS

During the period of Hyksos rule in Egypt (*ca.* 1720-1550 B.C.) the non-Semitic Hurrian people gained control of Ugarit.

They showed their anti-Egyptian feeling by smashing or mutilating Egyptian monuments and removing from them all references to Egypt. The Hurrians sought to strengthen ties with the Tigris-Euphrates area, but the prosperity of Ugarit suffered a temporary eclipse.

Few records have survived from the period of Hurrian dominance in Ugarit. The city seems to have lost its strategic importance for a time. Following the expulsion of the Hyksos from Egypt (ca. 1550 B.C.), Pharaohs Thutmosis I and II marched northward to gain effective control of Syria. Since Ugarit was the best port in Syria it was a prime objective of the Egyptians and by the time of Amenophis II (ca. 1435-1414 B.C.) an Egyptian garrison was stationed there. An inscription from Karnak in Egypt tells how Amenophis II when returning from a campaign in Mitanni found it necessary to hasten to Ugarit. The Egyptians brought stability to the Ugaritic economy and the city prospered.

EGYPTO-HURRIAN RULE

The Egyptians and the Hurrians of Ugarit reconciled their differences and united to meet a new threat from the Hittites. Egypt and the Hurrian state of Mittani were allies from 1440 to 1380 B.C., and even after the defeat of Mitanni by the Hittite king Suppiluliuma (1375-1340 B.C.), the Hittites did not molest Ugarit for several decades. The fifteenth and the fourteenth centuries B.C. were the golden age of Ugaritic history. Commerce was conducted without interruption both on land and sea, and a large population enjoyed a high living standard. Syrians, Cypriotes, Cretans, Achaeans, Hurrians, and Egyptians lived together peaceably in Ugarit.

Archaeology has thrown considerable light on the Ugarit of this period. Palace archives in Ugaritic and other languages provide the scholar with contemporary source material. It was during Ugarit's golden age that the great epics were written.

UGARITIC RULERS

Niqmad I and Yaqarum I are said to have ruled Ugarit during the nineteenth and eighteenth centuries B.C., but we have no records from this period. The successors of these early rulers did rule without interruption from the fourteenth century until the end of Ugaritic power (ca. 1200 B.C.).

Royal correspondence discovered at Ras Shamra mentions golden vessels and other items which Niqmad II sent to the

Hittite ruler, Suppiluliuma. While paying tribute to the Hittites, Niqmad also maintained an alliance with Egypt. An alabaster vase discovered during the 1952 excavations contains a hieroglyphic inscription identifying Niqmad as "ruler of Ugarit." It depicts a royal marriage scene which appears to be that of Niqmad and an Egyptian princess. Ugarit was caught between two great powers — Egypt and the Hittites — and each sought to control her. Ugarit seems to have been quite successful in her efforts to placate the rivals and maintain peaceful relations with both.

The Ugaritic epics, transmitted orally for centuries, were probably written during the reign of Niqmad II. It was during his reign (ca. 1360 B.C.) that Ugarit was destroyed by fire. The king of Tyre sent a letter to Amenophis IV (Akhenaten) of Egypt saying:

> And Ugarit, the royal city, has been destroyed
> by fire.
> Half of the city has been burned.
> The other half is not there!

After the fire the city seems quickly to have recovered its prosperity. It was under Hittite domination for a time but came under Egyptian control with Ramesses II (ca. 1290-1224 B.C.). Niqmad II of Ugarit was succeeded by his son Arhalpa who died childless. Toward the close of the fourteenth century, Arhalpa's brother Niqmepa took the throne, being succeeded in the early thirteenth century by Ammistamar II, who is known to have married an Amorite princess Ahat-Milku. The records speak of an expensive trousseau which she received as a wedding present.

During the reign of Niqmepa or Ammistamar II a fire destroyed a portion of the palace. Mursilis II was king of the Hittites at the time, and an ax bearing his name was found among the ruins of the palace. The Hittites evidently were responsible for the fire.

The reign of Ammistamar II was marked by growing trade with Crete. A text discovered in 1952 mentions a royal grant to a man named Sinaranu who was permitted to import grain, wine, and oil without interference. It contains the interesting line, "The inspector will not approach his house." Evidently there were customs regulations which were regularly enforced but certain importers were granted special privileges.

Ammistamar II was succeeded by Ibirana, and he by Niqmad III. Another ruler bearing the name Hammurabi is known, but his relation to the Niqmad dynasty is uncertain.

INTERNATIONAL RELATIONS

Situated in northern Syria, Ugarit was close to the Hittite Empire yet she wished to maintain trade and diplomatic relations with Egypt. Although largely successful, tensions between the Hittites and the Egyptians became acute during the fourteenth and thirteenth centuries and Ugarit was caught in the middle. Niqmad II had married an Egyptian princess but he continued to pay tribute to the Hittites. Ammistamar proclaimed himself "faithful servant" of the Hittites and at the same time gave gifts to Pa'ahu, a "man of Egypt."

It became necessary, however, after 1360 B.C. for Ugarit to acknowledge Hittite suzerainty. Ugaritic kings paid tribute and were as a rule not molested. Ugaritic soldiers fought with the Hittites against Ramesses II at the Battle of Kadesh (1276 B.C.). Still, Ugarit tried to maintain friendly relations with Egypt. An alabaster vase which was a gift of Ramesses II was found among the palace ruins at Ugarit, yet a Babylonian text explicitly states that Ugarit was under Hittite jurisdiction. A seal of the Hittite king Mursilis II, also found in the palace, indicates the presence of a Hittite ambassador there. Hittites sought and received special benefits at Ugarit, including exemption from the payment of customs duties. An Akkadian tablet from Ugarit contains a letter from the Hittite king Hattusilis III (ca. 1275-1250 B.C.) concerning the status of Hittite merchants in Ugarit.

After the Battle of Kadesh, fought to determine whether Hittites or Egyptians would control Syria, Ugarit enjoyed its final period of prosperity. Early in the thirteenth century Ugarit and Egypt are known to have enjoyed cordial relations. A stele found in the ruins of the Baal temple tells of a royal Egyptian scribe named Mami who was evidently an ambassador in the service of Pharaoh at Ugarit.

We learn from an Assyrian letter discovered at Ras Shamra that Ugarit was governed by a queen during the thirteenth century. Ugarit was friendly with Assyria at the time. Towards the end of the thirteenth century and the beginning of the twelfth century, northern Syria was overrun by "Sea People," a term used in Egyptian writings to describe invaders from the Balkans and the plains north of the Black Sea who entered northern Syria and pushed southward. It is probable that many of the Aegean, Mycenaean, and Cypriote inhabitants of Ugarit sought refuge in their native lands at the time. We have no record of the battle, but we know that the Sea Peoples destroyed Ugarit.

Economic as well as political reasons help account for the end of Ugaritic history *ca.* 1200 B.C. About that time iron began to replace copper as the metal used in the manufacture of tools and weapons. As long as Western Asia needed copper, Ugarit remained a strategic port because of its proximity to the copper-rich island of Cyprus. When copper was no longer needed, Ugarit lost its importance.

After the destruction of Ugarit, the port city never regained its ancient position. There are some evidences of occupation during the tenth century and Greek merchants of the sixth and fifth centuries are known to have stopped there. It was they who named the port *Leucos Limen,* "white harbor." A large number of archaic Greek coins dating to the second half of the sixth century has been found. Later settlements, however, were insignificant and the site was used for farming until the spectacular discovery in 1929.

A Cuneiform Dictionary from Ugarit. Types of ships are listed in two languages: Sumerian (left) and Akkadian (right).

III

A NEW ALPHABET AND A NEW LANGUAGE

In a corner of one of the rooms excavated during the 1929 campaign at Ras Shamra, a number of cuneiform tablets were discovered under a pile of ashes and rubble. When additional tablets came to light during the excavations of 1930 and 1932, scholars concluded that this room had been used as a library and a school for scribes.

Some of the tablets were written in Akkadian cuneiform signs — The syllabic system of writing on clay tablets which had been introduced into the area north of the Persian Gulf around 3000 B.C. and later disseminated throughout the Near East. First used by the non-Semitic Sumerians, the cuneiform syllabary was adapted to the Semitic Akkadian language used in Assyria and Babylonia which became the lingua franca of the Near East during the fifteenth and fourteenth centuries before Christ. The Amarna Letters, accidentally discovered in Egypt in 1887, were written by kings of city states in Syria and Palestine in Akkadian cuneiform.

Other tablets from Ras Shamra were found to have been written in a previously unknown type of cuneiform. The first of these enigmatic texts was published by Charles Virolleaud, then Director of Archaeological Works in Syria and the Lebanon, in the Spring, 1930 issue of the journal *Syria*. Scholars immediately attempted to decipher this strange new writing. Since the number of different signs was comparatively few — only thirty, as compared with the hundreds of signs in the Akkadian syllabary — they surmised that the Ugaritic texts were written in an alphabetic rather than a syllabic writing system.

Virolleaud, who had published the first texts, and Edouard Dhorme of the École Biblique in Jerusalem were among the first scholars who attempted to decipher the newly found tablets. Pioneer work was also done by Hans Bauer of the University of Halle. Dhorme and Bauer both had experience in cryptanalysis during World War I. The French government decorated Dhorme for breaking an enemy code at Salonika.

The work of decipherment began with much trial and error, but the scholars made a series of guesses which proved to be largely correct. Bauer surmised that the language of Ras Shamra might be Semitic, and this hypothesis proved to be the most valuable clue to the decipherment of the texts. He began by carefully tabulating the prefixes, the suffixes, and the single

1	a	16	m
2	e(i)	17	n
3	u	18	s
4	b	19	s_2
5	g	20	'
6	d	21	ġ
7	h	22	ṗ
8	w	23	ṣ
9	z	24	ẓ
10	ḥ	25	q
11	ḫ	26	r
12	ṭ	27	š
13	y	28	ṯ
14	k	29	t
15	l	30	ṯ

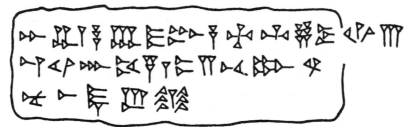

The Ugaritic Alphabet. Above: the cuneiform characters with their alphabetic equivalent. Below: an example of Ugaritic writing.

letter words he might expect to find in a West Semitic language. Then he studied the frequency and the position of the various signs in the texts, and, by cryptanalysis, found the values of certain of the letters.

When a prefix was found before a combination of letters which appeared to be a name, Bauer assumed that this would be the West Semitic preposition "l" meaning "to." In a list of names Bauer noted that two letters recurred and he correctly surmised that they were "b" and "n" comprising the word for son (*bn*). The word for king (*mlk*) was easily identified. With his "b" and "l" Bauer readily identified the word *b'l*, the Canaanite god Baal.

As the work progressed false identifications were bound to be made, for Ugaritic is a language in its own right and not a mere dialect of Hebrew or some other West Semitic language. Edouard Dhorme, who was working independently on the decipherment of the Ugaritic texts, produced results which largely agreed with those of Bauer. He was able, moreover, to eliminate some errors which had crept into Bauer's work. The two scholars published practically identical lists of the values of the Ugaritic characters.

It seems to be a matter of academic justice that the final refinements in the identification of the Ugaritic alphabetic characters came from the labors of Charles Virolleaud who had first published the tablets and permitted his fellow scholars around the world to test their wits on them. In 1931, a year after the first publication of texts in an unknown language, Virolleaud published in *Syria* his translation of "The Epic of Aleyan and Mot," a fragment of Semitic mythology which was to show the relevance of Ugarit to Semitic studies. In subsequent years a vast corpus of Ugaritic literature was to be translated and analyzed.

Two of the Ras Shamra tablets (one of which is defective) list in order the letters of the Ugaritic alphabet. Twenty-two of the Ugaritic letters have the same values as the corresponding letters of the Hebrew alphabet, and they are arranged in the order familiar to students of Hebrew. The eight signs which do not appear in Hebrew are inserted at appropriate points in the Ugaritic alphabet.

We cannot account for the origin of the Ugaritic alphabet. Many scholars feel that it was invented by someone who adapted the familar cuneiform method of syllabic writing to a less cumbersome alphabetic system. We know that the alphabet spread beyond Ugaritic for an oval plaque in the same script has been discovered at 'Ain Shems in Palestine.

Once the alphabet was deciphered, scholars were able to study the Ugaritic texts which had already been published and they were prepared to cope with the new material which came to light in subsequent excavations. The name "Ugaritic" came to be used of both the alphabet and the language of the texts. Semitists began the scientific study of the Ugaritic language and numerous attempts were made to determine its linguistic affinities. At various times it has been associated with the Canaanite, Amorite, Arabic, South Arabic, or even Akkadian languages, but no classification has gained general acceptance.

Much of the vocabulary of the Ugaritic texts is similar to that of the Old Testament. Hebrew poetry, which generally preserves archaic forms, is closer in grammatical structure to Ugaritic than is the prose of the Bible. The definite article, lacking in Ugaritic, is frequently omitted from Hebrew poetry. The Hebrew *waw consecutive,* regularly used in Biblical prose, is rare in Ugaritic. It is totally absent from Psalm 68, an example of Hebrew poetry which has many parallels to the Ugaritic literature.

The study of Ugaritic has been greatly facilitated by the writings of Cyrus H. Gordon. His *Ugaritic Manual* includes a grammar of the language, the transliteration of the major texts, and a glossary. Some knowledge of Ugaritic is indispensable in the proper understanding of the history and literature of the Old Testament.

IV

THE GODS OF UGARIT

The religion described in the Ugaritic epics had many points in common with that of the Canaanites which was consistently denounced by the prophets of Israel. Ugarit looked upon the great God El as the father of seventy *elim* or gods which comprised the Ugaritic pantheon. A stele discovered at Ras Shamra shows El seated upon a throne, receiving an offering from the king of Ugarit. El is of mature years and majestic in appearance.

El. A plaque depicts El, the father-god of the Canaanite pantheon, receiving an offering from the King of Ugarit.

The epics indicate that he was the final arbiter in disputes among the gods, but in general he was inactive. He bears the epithet "father of years" and, as an older deity, appears to have turned over most routine matters to the younger gods who were more popular than El in the actual cult.

In Ugaritic mythology El's wife bore the name Athirat or Elat and she served as the mother goddess of the pantheon. Her name appears in the form Asherah in the Old Testament, a word which was translated "groves" thirty-nine times in the King James Version (cf. Judg. 3:7; II Kings 23:4). The Asherim (plural of Asherah) of Scripture, were the female cult objects which corresponded to the male objects of the infamous Baal cult.

Of the seventy sons and daughters of El and Athirat, both the Ugaritic mythology and the Old Testament indicate that Baal became the most popular. He was the fertility god who rode upon the clouds and was responsible for the rains which brought life to be parched soil of Canaan. A Ras Shamra stele depicts him with a mace in his right hand and a thunderbolt in his left hand. Baal is sometimes designated as "Zebul (Prince), Lord of the Earth." He earlier bore the name of Hadad, the god whose presence was apparent in the violent storms of autumn and winter. At Ugarit he was often designated as Aliyan Baal, an expression which probably means "Baal, the Mighty One."

The Biblical name Baal-zebub, the god of Ekron (II Kings 1:2) appears to be an intentional corruption of the name Baal-Zebul. Baal-zebub is, by definition, "the lord of flies." The Pharisees of New Testament times spoke of Beelzebub (AV, NEB) or Beelzebul (RSV) as "the prince of the devils" (Matt. 12:24). The Nestle edition of the Greek Text of the New Testament prefers the reading Beelzebul. The similarity between Beelzebul and the Canaanite Baal-zebul has caused many scholars to see in the reading Beelzebub an intentional corruption in the name whereby the original "princely Baal" of the Canaanites was contemptuously named the "lord of flies" by the Israelites. Since the gods of the heathen were identified with demons, "princely Baal" became a name for Satan, the prince of demons.

The term Aliyan Baal is frequently used in the epics to describe Baal as the god of fertility in his conflicts with Mot, the god of death. We also read of an encounter between Baal and the seven-headed monster Lotan who is the Ugaritic monster of the deep. The Hebrew Leviathan is a variant of the name Lotan, although in the Bible Leviathan becomes a symbol of evil and is vanquished by Yahweh, the God of Israel.

The **Storm God.** A limestone stele from Ugarit depicts Baal with a raised club in his right hand. His left hand leans on a spear. The top of the spear is in the shape of lightning, or a sacred tree.

Anat. Sister and consort of Baal, Anat was goddess of love and war.

The sister and consort of Baal was "the Virgin Anat." When Baal was driven from the earth, Anat mourned for him and finally enlisted the aid of the sun-goddess in bringing him back from the nether world. Anat was also the goddes of war. The Aqhat Epic recounts the tragic circumstances which followed when a bow which had been made for Anat was accidentally misplaced. The Biblical Judge Shamgar is termed "son of Anat(h)" (Judg. 3:31; 5:6). Since Anat was a goddess of war, the term could mean "Shamgar the warrior." The plural form of Anat, Anathoth, is the name of the suburb of Jerusalem which was the home of Jeremiah (Jer. 1:1; 32:7). The plural form may have indicated the presence of a number of Anat(h) idols there. W. F. Albright suggests that the form Anathoth exhibits a tendency to encompass a variety of virtues and attributes in one deity — a tendency toward monotheism which found its highest expression in the Hebrew *Elohim.*

Although the Ugaritic literature makes it clear that El and Athirat were husband and wife, it may be significant that the Bible presents Baal and Athirat (or Asherah) as counterparts.

Kapelrud notes that Athirat was already in the process of becoming Baal's consort in the Ugaritic texts: "The first goddess of the pantheon must be the consort of the first god, and as Baal, apparently slowly, drove out El from the leading place, he also took over his wife" (Arvid S. Kapelrud, *Baal in the Ras Shamra Texts*, pp. 77-78).

In addition to the goddesses Athirat and Anat, the name of Athtart appears in the Ugaritic texts and in a wide area of the Middle East. The Biblical form of the word is Ashtoreth and its plural, Ashtaroth occurs nine times in the Old Testament (cf. Judg. 2:13). Athtart entered the Greek world through Cyprus and became the Astarte — Aphrodite of classical mythology. In Greece as in the Canaanite world she was a goddess of generation and fertility.

The Fertility Goddess (Athtart— Astarte). The nude goddess is depicted on a gold pendant discovered at Ras Shamra.

Like Anat, Athtart was a goddess of war as well as love. Twice the Ugaritic texts invoke her to break the skull of an adversary. Ishtar, the Assyro-Babylonian counterpart to Athtart, was known as "lady of battles, valiant among goddesses." She is depicted with a bow in her hands, standing on a chariot drawn by seven lions. Following the defeat of the Israelite armies at Mount Gilboa, the Philistines deposited the armor of the slain king, Saul, in the temple of Ashtaroth (Athtart). This act, described in I Samuel 31:10, underscores the warlike character of the goddess. After gaining a victory on the battlefield, her devotees brought the trophies of victory to her temple.

Youthful Athtar was the god who attempted to occupy the throne of Baal while the fertility god was absent in the nether world. The Baal Epic designates him "Athtar, the terrible" (Baal III, i, 26-28). He was manifest in Venus, the bright morning star and, according to Theodor Gaster, was the deity responsible for irrigation (*Thespis*, p. 198).

Although Athtar does not occupy a prominent place in the Ugaritic texts, he reappears in the compound name Athtar-Chemosh as the national god of Moab in the Mesha inscription (9th century B.C.). One of the ancient names for Athtar was *mlk*, "the king," a name which appears as Milcom, the god of Ammon (I Kings 11:5, 33), and Molech, the god to whom idolatrous Israelites offered their children in sacrifice (Lev. 18:21; 20:2, 3, 4; Jer. 32:35). A passage from the *Life of St. Nilus*, written in the fifth century A.D., tells of a Bedouin raid on the monasteries of Sinai during which Nilus and his son were taken captive. The Bedouin intended to offer the son, Theodulus, as a sacrifice to the Venus star although, providentially, he escaped.

The Ugaritic texts do not specifically mention human sacrifices to Athtar, although the epithet "the terrible" would be appropriate for a deity who required them. Athtar in the Baal Epic was short of stature and unable to occupy the throne of Baal who ultimately returned from the nether world and ruled in his own right.

In view of the fact that the gods had to travel over vast distances, and that they often communicated with the world of men, they found it necessary to have messengers. Gupan and Ugar performed this function for the great gods of Ugarit. One of their most important journeys was that which took them from Mot (the god of death) to Baal. The message which they carried precipitated Baal's journey to the nether world.

The god who bore the compound name Kathir-and-Khasis is mentioned over forty times in the texts. He was the god of arts and crafts and served as the master builder at Ugarit. It was his responsibility to fashion temples for the gods and to provide them with weapons. Obermann suggests that Kathir-and-Khasis represents the advance in technology, including new processes of smelting and molding, which revolutionized life when metals began to be used (Julian Obermann, *Ugaritic Mythology*, pp. 15-16). Kapelrud, however, argues that it was the master builder rather than the inventor who was honored in the ancient world (Arvid S. Kapelrud, *Baal in the Ras Shamra Tablets*, pp. 82-86).

Yam, god of the sea, also bore the name Lotan, Biblical Leviathan, and was identified with a seven-headed monster who was

the epitome of evil. Baal's victory over Lotan is paralleled by the
victories of Yahweh over Leviathan:

Thou didst divide the sea [*Yam*] by thy strength;
   thou breakest the heads of the dragons [*tanninim*] in the waters.
Thou breakest the heads of leviathan in pieces, and gavest him
   to be meat to the people inhabiting the wilderness (Ps. 74:13-14).

Sometimes this is presented in terms of an eschatological
battle:

In that day the Lord (*Yahweh*) with his sore and great and strong
sword shall punish leviathan, the piercing serpent, even leviathan,
that crooked serpent; and he shall slay the dragon that is in the sea
(Isa. 27:1).

The Ugaritic god of death was Mot, a powerful deity who frequently challenged the power of Baal. As Baal produced fertility and life, so Mot was responsible for sterility and death.
The two were opposites and at a given moment one or the other
might be on the throne. During times of famine, Mot reigned su-
preme. Some scholars see the annual dry season of Syria and
Palestine as a period when Mot was in control. Mot also bore the
names Resheph, "the ravager," and Horon, "he of the pit." Beth-
horon, in the valley of Aijalon, was probably a shrine to Horon
during the days of Canaanite occupation of the land. Resheph
was the god of plagues and pestilence.

The heavenly bodies were represented in the pantheon.
Shamash and Yareah served as the deities corresponding to the
sun and the moon. Shamash was also regarded as the god of
justice because he sees all things. Sedeq and Mishor, "right and
equity" were his ministers. Towns such as Beth-shemesh and
Jericho reflect times when the sun and moon were worshiped
as important deities in Canaan.

Dawn and Sunset were known as Shahar and Shalem and described in the Ugaritic texts as sons of El. Known as "the celestial
ones" they are comparable to Castor and Pollux of classical mythology. Offerings were also made to Queen Shapash (the sun goddess) and the stars. Shapash is the feminine counterpart to
Shamash.

Dagan, the Dagon of the Old Testament, is the god of grain
and the genius of the crops. He is sometimes described as father
of Baal, evidently reflecting a time when Dagan occupied a more
prominent place in the pantheon. The fact that Baal might appear as the son of either El or Dagan appears illogical to the
western mind, but consistency was not expected of ancient myths
and legends which could readily be adapted to varying circumstances. The largest of the temples excavated at Ugarit was
dedicated to Dagan.

The Biblical writers were aware of the Canaanite mythology and they sought to keep the people of Israel true to Yahweh, their god. Not only did prophets such as Elijah denounce the Baal cult, but there is also a subtle, yet effective, polemic against idolatry in the early chapters of Genesis. There it is made clear that God (*Elohim*) created all things — including sun, moon, and stars. The invention of arts and crafts is not attributed to the gods, but to humans of the line of Cain. Brass and iron work are said to have originated with Tubal-cain (Gen. 4:22).

The Canaanite deities, however, left their impress on the history and geography of the Holy Land. The Philistines took the sacred ark to the temple of Dagon (I Sam. 5:2-5). Beth-shemesh, Beth-horon, Anathoth, Jericho, and scores of other places witness to the polytheism which marked the land of Canaan before Israelite monotheism became a dominant force.

V

RELIGIOUS RITES IN ISRAEL AND UGARIT

In view of the wide variety of religious ritual in the Old Testament, from the simple, patriarchal offerings and prayers to the complex Temple worship, considerable restraint is needed in drawing parallels to the Ugaritic cultus. Among primitive peoples there is often a close relationship between myth and ritual but this is not always the case. Our knowledge of such relationships at Ugarit is scanty indeed. We know that myths often develop when artistic fantasy is coupled with religious interest. Etiological tales and matters which could be termed aesthetic, rather than formally religious, often have a place in the mythology of a people. The Ugaritic epics can be understood and enjoyed for their own sake, quite apart from any theory of cultic enactment or recital.

One of the controverted points of interpretation in the Ugartic literature concerns the relation of the Baal Epic to cult. Rejecting the idea that Baal represents a seasonal and cultic motif, Cyrus H. Gordon says:

> Every year with the onslaught of the summer draught, Baal is supposed to be killed by Mot, the god of death; and every year, Baal is revived with the return of the rains and fertility. The evidence for this is of the most specious character. The Adonis myth has an embellishment, known from Greek sources, to the effect that Zeus settled the rivalry of Persephone and Aphrodite over Adonis, by assigning the beautiful god part of every year to Persephone in the underworld, and the other part of every year to Aphrodite above. Before the discovery of the Ugaritic texts this Greek version was read back into Phoenician mythology, and now it is read still further back into Ugaritic mythology in clear opposition to the plain meaning of the Ugaritic texts.
>
> — *Ugaritic Literature*, pp. 3-4

Gordon insists that famine is not a seasonal phenomenon in Palestine. He interprets passages which speak of the failing or death of Baal in terms of an abnormally bad year, or a series of bad years. Thus a seven year famine, as in the Biblical account

36

of Joseph in Egypt, would imply an absence of Baal during the extended period.

R. De Langhe agrees that "the cycle of Aliyan Baal is essentially a series of poems with varied episodes from which liturgical or rubrical indications are totally absent" ("Myth, Ritual, and Kingship in the Ras Shamra Tablets," in *Myth, Ritual and Kingship*, S. H. Hooke, ed., p. 139). Although going farther than Gordon in suggesting the possibility of an annual, seasonal motif, De Langhe states that "it is not necessary to go beyond the theory of myth as an expression not of deeds and actions, but of ideas, hopes and aspirations" (*Ibid.*, p. 149).

Rejecting the seasonal interpretation of the Baal epic does not close Gordon's eyes to other cultic notices of an annual nature in Ugaritic literature. Text three speaks of an offering made by the king "on the day of the new moon." Gordon notes, "In the ancient East kings often took part in rituals; e.g., the New Year or Akitu festival in Babylon" (*op. cit.*, p. 108). He further suggests that the rulers of Ugarit may have been influenced by the Hittites in such matters.

Text nine actually speaks of an annual ritual performed by the king:

> The king washes himself of spittle the (second/two) month(s) of Tishri.

This tablet describes a ritual for the forgiveness of the soul made in the form of a sacrifice to the gods. Gordon notes, "Since the ritual is dated in Tishri (which is still the month of the autumnal or religious New Year among the Jews), this may be a New Year ritual" (*Ibid.*). Not only the New Year, but also the solemn Hebrew Day of Atonement takes place during Tishri.

Both the Biblical and the Ugaritic documents speak of a communion meal known as *shelamim*, traditionally translated, "peace offerings." Gray states, "The basic sense of the term ... is 'communion,' making whole (*sh-l-m*) of the relationship between the community and its God" (John Gray, *The Legacy of Canaan*, p. 144). Sacrifices designated *shelamim* were shared by the deity and his worshipers. The offering stressed the solidarity of the group and its relation to its deity. The god was regarded as a member of the family, sharing in its total life.

The Aqhat Epic in describing a faithful son notes the custom of *shelamim*. The son must:

> Support him (i.e., his father) when he is full of wine,
> ... eat his share in the temple of Baal
> Consume his portion in the temple of El (Aqhat II, i, 32-34).

In the Biblical records, the blood and fat of the *shelamîm* were highly regarded and consequently assigned as "the Lord's portion" (Lev. 3:1-17). Other portions were assigned to the officiating priests, and the remainder of the carcass of the sacrificial victim was given to the worshiper for a social feast. The temptress of Proverbs 7 used this meat of the *shelamîm* to attract her victim. She said:

> Sacrifices of *shelamîm* were due from me;
> This day have I paid my vows (Prov. 7:14).

Thereupon she assured the foolish youth that her husband was away on a journey and that they could enjoy the privacy of her house.

Much of the vocabulary associated with the Mosaic offerings was current in the Ugaritic literature. Among common words we meet the Ugaritic *dbh* which corresponds to the Hebrew *zbh*, "sacrifice." The words for gift (*mtn*) and vow (*ndr*) are the same in both languages. Ugaritic *sh'ly* "to offer" corresponds to Hebrew *h'lh*, literally "to cause to go up." The Ugaritic Burnt Offering (*shrp*), although using a different Semitic root is identical in function with Hebrew *'olh*, all of which was burned on the altar.

The sacrificial animals are also comparable. In Ugarit the offering may be an *'alp* ("ox") or *sh* ("sheep") which must be perfect (*tm*) and approved (*nkbd*). All of these stipulations have Biblical parallels. The basic difference is in the concept of deity. All Israelite sacrifices were to be offered to Yahweh, but the people of Ugarit brought offerings to El, Baal, Dagan, Athirat, Yam, and a host of other deities. The concept of atonement was present in Ugaritic terminology, however. Text 9 speaks of the purpose of a sacrifice as *slh npsh*, "forgiveness of soul."

In cult personnel, as in the sacrificial system itself, neither Israel nor Ugarit was static. In patriarchal times the tribal leader served as his own priest and as late as Saul an Israelite ruler felt justified in assuming priestly responsibilities. Saul was condemned for intrusion into the priestly office when he offered sacrifices (I Sam. 13:9; 14:35).

The epics of Keret and Aqhat describe priestly functions as performed by the kings Keret and Danel. If there were other ministrants they are not mentioned in the texts. Like Melchizedek, the kings named in the Ugaritic epics represented their people before the deity in a priestly ministry and represented the divine will to the people as ruler of the state. In a time of drought, King Danel embraced and kissed the various plants in order to promote their fertility (Aqhat I, ii, 1-26). We also know that Itto-baal of Sidon served as both king and priest of Athtart

(Astarte). Mesha of Moab is said to have offered his oldest son as a sacrifice (II Kings 3:27).

After the giving of the Mosaic Law, Israel limited its priesthood to the Aaronic family of the tribe of Levi. Thus the concept of a priest-king such as Melchizedek was missing from post-Mosaic Israel, save in Messianic prophecy (Ps. 110:4). Ugarit, too, seems to have developed a class of cultic functionaries for we read of *khnm* ("priests") and *qdshm* ("consecrated persons").

A colophon appended to Text 62 indicates that the priest was custodian of tradition and authority. He it was who produced the sacred literature:

> The narrator is Atn-Prln, chief of the priests (and) chief of the herdsmen, the T'-ite.
> (Dated in the reign of) Nqmd, king of Ugarit, Master of Yrgh, Lord of Trmn.

The context indicates that Atn-Prln taught *(lmd)* the myth to a scribe who identified himself as 'Il-Mlk. This may be interpreted to mean that the texts were preserved in both oral and written forms and that the priests had the prime responsibility for their preservation.

Many aspects of Canaanite worship were repulsive to the leaders of Israel's religious life. Israel was warned not to adopt the customs of the Canaanites (Lev. 18:3), and Israelite prophets consistently denounced the Baal cult. In basic vocabulary, however, the rites of the two peoples had much in common. There is no evidence of borrowing on the part of Israel or the Canaanites of Ugarit. Similarities are doubtless the result of the common Semitic background of both peoples.

VI

SOCIAL LIFE IN UGARIT AND IN THE OLD TESTAMENT

Both the Ugaritic documents and the Hebrew Scriptures present a variety of approaches toward social institutions. Within the Bible we meet a complete spectrum of social life from the semi-nomadism of the patriarchs to the centralized monarchy of Solomon.

Ugaritic society, as we know it, was headed by a hereditary king who ruled with divine authority. He was not, like the Egyptian Pharaohs, a god in his own right. The epics describe the kings as suckled by the goddesses Athirat and Anat, and thus endowed with supernatural strength. Priestesses of Canaanite goddesses may have actually suckled the children of kings.

The ideal king was one who dispensed justice. Of righteous Danel we read:

> He rises to take his seat at the opening of the gate
> In the place of the notables who are in the public place.
> He decides the case of the widow,
> He judges the suit of the orphan, (Aqhat II, v, 6-8).

The Biblical writers also exhibit a concern for widows and orphans. It is said of God that He "doth execute the judgment of the fatherless and widow, and loveth the stranger, in giving him food and raiment" (Deut. 10:17; cf. Ps. 68:5). In a day of spiritual laxity, Isaiah complained: "Thy princes are rebellious, and companions of thieves: every one loveth gifts and followeth after rewards: they judge not the fatherless, neither doth the cause of the widow come unto them" (Isa. 1:23).

During the period of the Israelite monarchy there was a real distinction between "state" and "church." Each had its own functionaries, all of whom were subject to the law and will of Yahweh. Samuel anointed Saul as Israel's first king, but Saul was severely censured when he presumed to offer sacrifices (I Sam. 13:8-15). The king was not permitted to usurp the functions of the priest. Subsequently, when Saul decided to spare Agag, counter to Yahweh's word through Samuel, a permanent rupture ensued and young David was anointed to succeed rebellious Saul (I Sam. 15:9-23; 16:12-13). When David sinned in the episode involving Bathsheba and Uriah, the prophet Nathan came to his king with a word of judgment (II Sam. 11:1 — 12:14). After the division of the kingdom we read how Ahab's judicial murder of Naboth so stirred the wrath of Elijah that he pronounced the doom of the reigning dynasty (I Kings 21:1-24). Kings were regarded as the elect of Yahweh but they were required to obey the divine law.

In Ugarit, although the King had both privilege and responsibility, we do not know of any external checks which were placed upon him. There is no evidence of a codified system of law in Canaan comparable with those of Babylon, Assyria, the Hittites, and Israel. During the period reflected in the Keret and Aqhat epics the king appears to have rendered judgments on the basis of his own wisdom and his feeling for the good of the people. He appears to have combined in himself the functions of king, priest, and mediator of divine revelation.

The administrative texts from Ugarit exhibit a highly organized system of fiscal control. The population was organized into districts, each of which was required to provide either silver or services for the royal projects. Other texts speak of payments made by families which were grouped as guilds.

Israelite political life was reorganized by Solomon who divided the nation into twelve administrative districts, evidently disregarding the older tribal divisions (I Kings 4:1-19). Officers were appointed to exact both taxes and forced labor from each. Solomon's economic policies, however, brought the nation to the verge of bankruptcy. In payment for obligations incurred in his building projects, Solomon actually handed over Israelite territory to Hiram of Tyre (I Kings 9:11-14). Israel was forced to bear an intolerable tax burden with the result that the nation split into two rival factions shortly after Solomon's death.

Ugarit developed a caste system which differed markedly from the social life of Israel. Aryan invasions of northern Syria seem to have left their mark on the culture of that area, whereas Israel was more isolated. John Gray writes:

> While in many respects Canaanite society reflects conditions of the tribes of the desert hinterland, it is equally true that Ugarit in particular, in the extreme North of Canaan, bore the impact of invasion of non-Semitic elements from the North and East, particularly of the Aryans who penetrated the area and imposed themselves as a military aristocracy on the native population about the

end of the nineteenth century. It is our opinion that the classification of the population of Ugarit by vocations is a reflection of the caste system associated with the Aryans of India.

— *The Legacy of Canaan*, p. 166

Israel, to be sure, had a priestly caste (the Levites), but there are few other hints of vocational distinctions in Israelite society. Ugarit, however, had at least eight distinct castes as recorded on Text 400.

High in the social structure at Ugarit were the military castes. The first of these appears in the texts of *mrynm*, a term known from Egyptian inscriptions where the *mariannu* appear as specialists in chariot warfare (cf. J. H. Breasted, *Ancient Records of Egypt*, II, p. 590). Aryan invaders are thought to have introduced the horse and the two-wheeled chariot into Western Asia as an instrument of war about 1800 B.C. The chariot-riding *mariannu* owed both their status and their loyalty to the king who appointed them. Although caste connotations are not present, Scripture does reflect the personal relationship between the Israelite king and his army. We read that when Saul saw "any strong man, or any valiant man, he took him unto him" (I Sam. 14:52). David served under Achish of Gath in such a capacity (I Sam. 27:1-12).

Among other military castes in Ugarit, mention is made of the *hpt*, a term which appears in the Amarna Tablets as *hubshu*. Rib-Addi of Byblos mentions the *hubshu* as a serious menace to his power. He complained that they gave up their children and property in order to get food. They plundered cities and were as great a menace to the king as his avowed enemies (cf. J. A. Knudtzon, *Die El-Amarna Tafeln*, 85:12, 114:21). Power in their hands enabled them to rebel against the king they had pledged to serve.

The exact meaning of the term *hpt* is problematical. Albright suggests as a primary meaning "a serf bound to the land," with the secondary sense of "a peasant landholder or freeholder." In the latter sense the word entered the Hebrew vocabulary.

When Israel was challenged by the Philistines, Saul offered a reward to anyone who would rescue Israel from the giant Goliath:

> ...and it shall be that the man who killeth him, the king will enrich him with great riches, and will give him his daughter, and make his father's house free *(hopshi)* in Israel (I Sam. 17:25).

The individual honored in this way would be released from local and family responsibilities and would enjoy the status of a feudatory to the king (cf. John Gray, *op. cit.*, p. 170). The relationship became hereditary, so that the *hopshi* could develop into a large and powerful segment of society.

The concept of community responsibility played an important part in the life of Israel, and it is also an important element in Ugaritic culture. In a tribal society, the interests of the group take precedence over those of the individual. The concept of blood revenge, so common in ancient societies, is a case in point. In the absence of a strong central government the family became the means of enforcing the moral code. When a murder was committed, the relatives of the deceased sought vengeance. The family of the murderer is considered to be a unit, however, and the concept of "a life for a life" can apply to any member of a murderer's family — to the fifth generation.

Corporate responsibility is frequently stressed in Scripture. We read that "... Achan took of the *herem* and the anger of Yahweh was kindled against the children of Israel" (Josh. 7:1 — 8:29). Achan took for himself that which was to be devoted to Yahweh. The whole Israelite army thereupon was defeated in battle because of one man's sin. Subsequent victory was possible only after the culprit and his family were stoned.

The "redeemer" (*go'el*) in Israel had a twofold function, related in each instance to the corporate concept of society. It was his responsibility to avenge the murder of a kinsman, but he was also expected to redeem (i.e., buy back) property which belonged in the family unit. Boaz, in the story of Ruth, served as *go'el* in this latter sense.

After Absalom had killed his half-brother Amnon, the wise woman of Tekoah tried to effect a reconciliation between David and Absalom. She appealed to the king by means of fictitious testimony:

> I am indeed a widow woman, and mine husband is dead. And thy handmaid had two sons, and they strove together in the field, and there was none to part them, but the one smote the other, and slew him. And, behold the whole family is risen against thine handmaid, and they said, Deliver him that smote his brother that we may kill him, for the life of his brother whom he slew; and we will destroy the heir also: and so they shall quench my coal which is left, and shall not leave to my husband either name or remainder upon the earth (II Sam 14·4-7)

The woman told her story to impress upon David the necessity of forgiving Absalom. It stresses the necessity of preserving the "name" of a deceased husband. The woman's story, however, underscores the possibility that social standards and aims may conflict with one another. Society recognized the desirability of preserving the family name, and also the desirability of killing the manslayer. In this instance, to have done the second would have rendered the first impossible.

The wise woman actually appealed to David as king. She assumed that his office would make it possible for him to abrogate the demands of social custom if he had good reasons for doing so. Before the monarchy there was no effective check on social custom and "every man did that which was right in his own eyes" (Judg. 21:25).

The concept of blood revenge appears in the Ugaritic epics. The sister of the dead hero of the Aqhat text assumed the role of go'el. She said:

> I will smite him who smote my brother,
> I will make an end of him who annihilated the
>   child of my mother (Aqhat I, iv, 31-35).

When a corpse was discovered with no trace of the murderer, the Deuteronomic law assigned a corporate responsibility to the community nearest to the scene of the crime. The elders of the community were required to swear innocence over the blood of an heifer slain in a perennial stream (Deut. 21:1-9). Theodor H. Gaster suggests that such a custom is illustrated in Ugarit when Danel cursed three communities upon learning of the death of his son Aqhat (*Thespis,* p. 302).

Ugarit was a maritime state and enjoyed cultural interchange with the islands of the Mediterranean, Asia Minor, Egypt, and the Tigris-Euphrates valley. Israel had relatively poor seaports and was isolated from the main arteries of communication. In large measure the ideas of Israel's prophetic leaders found no parallel elsewhere. Much of the cultural framework, however, was held in common by the Semitic peoples of the ancient Near East.

VII

THE UGARITIC EPICS

Of several hundred Ugaritic texts which have been studied, none are of greater interest than the three major epics discovered in the library of Ugarit and dated during the reign of King Niqmad II. Since Niqmad is known to have paid tribute to the Hittite king, Suppiluliuma (1375-1340 B.C.), our copies of the epics date from the fourteenth century B.C., although it is probable that they existed in earlier recensions. Like epics of other Peoples, they probably were passed on by word of mouth for centuries.

The Aqhat Epic

One of the heroes described in the Ugaritic texts was named Danel. His life approximated the Biblical ideal in that he defended the widows and protected the orphans. Although blessed with a daughter, righteous Danel had no son, a matter of serious concern in the Biblical as well as the Ugaritic milieu (Gen. 15:2). The desire for a male child took Danel to the temple, where he spent seven days as a servant. On the seventh day the god Baal took pity on Danel and announced that his prayer would be answered. Thereupon Danel spent seven more days in celebrating the good news that he was to become the father of a son. In due time the child Aqhat was born.

Danel's quest for a son has interesting Biblical parallels. Abraham was so concerned that he have a son that, according to the Biblical narrative (Gen. 16:1-16), he resorted to the expedient of having a child by his wife's handmaid, Hagar. This practice, so foreign to modern thought, is attested both in the Nuzi letters and in the code of Hammurabi.

Not only did Danel pray for a son, but also he spent seven days in the temple to win the favor of his god. This is analagous to the rite of incubation which was commonly practiced in ancient

45

The Aqhat Epic. This clay tablet, inscribed with alphabetic cuneiform characters, contains part of the story of Aqhat, the son of Danel, whose death resulted in a seven year famine.

times. Individuals who craved a favor from the gods would go to a temple and sleep within its precincts. Dreams experienced under those circumstances were thought to reveal the purposes of the gods. In this instance the god Baal revealed to Danel the good news that his prayer would be answered.

The annunciation of the birth of a son to Danel has many Biblical parallels. An angel declared to Abraham, "Sarah thy wife shall have a son" (Gen. 18:14). Samson was heralded by "the angel of the Lord" who gave instructions concerning his mother's conduct and that which would be expected of the lad (Judg. 13:3-5). Annunciations occur in the New Testament before the births of John the Baptist (Luke 1:13) and Jesus (Luke 1:31).

After the birth of Aqhat, Danel took a secondary place in the epic. He did, however, have opportunity to entertain the god Kathir-and-Khasis who stopped at Danel's home while traveling northward from Egypt. Kathir-and-Khasis was the divine smith of the Ugaritic pantheon, serving the same function as Haphaestus in classical mythology and Vulcan among the Norsemen. The Egyptian god of arts and crafts, Ptah, was identified with Kathir-and-Khasis. The seat of Ptah-worship was the Egyptian city of

Memphis, and there the Canaanite Kathir-and-Khasis had his forge.

Danel's entertainment of Kathir-and-Khasis may be compared with that of Abraham who made generous provision for "three men" who visited him at Mamre (Gen. 18:2-33). As Danel ordered his wife Danitiya to prepare a meal for his guests, (Aqhat II, v, 12-32) so Abraham instructed Sarah to prepare a suitable meal for his guests, one of whom was later identified with the deity (Gen. 18:1-15).

When Kathir-and-Khasis continued his journey northward he accidentally left behind a bow and arrow which, we later learn, had been made expressly for Anat, goddess of love and war. Danel innocently gave the bow to his son Aqhat with the reminder that the first thing which he killed with it belonged to the gods. The "law of firstfruits" is common to Biblical usage (Exod. 23:19; Lev. 23:10; Deut. 18:4), and is here seen to have been observed in Ugarit.

The epic next revolves around the attempt of Anat to secure from Aqhat the bow which had been originally made for her. As the bow flashed like lightning across the waters, Anat spied it and dashed to the ground the cup from which she had been drinking. She hastened to Aqhat and offered him as much silver and gold as he might demand in exchange for the bow. Aqhat, however, made the prosaic observation that materials for making a bow and arrow were plentiful. Anat, reasoned Aqhat, could easily ask Kathir-and-Khasis to make a new bow for her.

When the offer of silver and gold fell on deaf ears, Anat offered to make Aqhat immortal if he would but give her the coveted weapons. The offer of life as long as that of "Baal son of El" did not impress Aqhat, however. To him the offer appeared ludicrous for he did not know he was talking to a goddess. Anat had appeared in the form of a young lady, and Aqhat accused her of deception. Old age and death are the lot of all men, and the offer of a means of avoiding them could not be taken seriously.

The motif of man's accidental loss of immortality is not uncommon in ancient literature. The Gilgamesh Epic tells how its hero actually secured a plant which would insure perpetual youth, only to drop it into the water where it was eaten by the serpent. The Biblical account of man in Eden is on a different level, however. Although the motif — man's loss of immortality — is present, the moral element in the Biblical narrative stands in contrast to the arbitrariness of its parallels in ancient literature. In the Biblical account man does not lose immortality through an accident, but by a willful act of rebellion against his Creator.

The serpent suggested that man, by eating the forbidden fruit, would be like the gods, "knowing good and evil" (Gen. 3:5). Man disobeyed God and was expelled from paradise.

When Aqhat persisted in his refusal to part with the bow, Anat went to her father El, asking him to intervene. El agreed, and Anat hired a ruffian named Yatpun to get the bow by force. Anat proposed to change Yatpun into an eagle (or hawk) who would associate with a flock of birds hovering over the place where Aqhat was eating. It would be Yatpun's responsibility to strike Aqhat, rendering him unconscious, and thus recover the bow for Anat. The plan was carried out but much to the grief of Anat, Aqhat was killed. To add to the tragedy of the whole episode, Yatpun accidentally dropped the bow into the sea where it was irretrievably lost. The shedding of innocent blood resulted in a parched earth, and the bow was gone forever.

The concept of innocent blood polluting the ground finds a parallel in the Biblical story of Cain and Abel. As part of the curse pronounced upon Cain, God said, "When thou tillest the ground it shall not henceforth yield unto thee its strength" (Gen. 4:12). Following the death of Saul and Jonathan, David prayed as recorded in II Samuel 1:21:

> Ye mountains of Gilboa
> let there be no dew nor rain upon you,
> neither upsurging of the deep.

The language which David employed in this dirge is strikingly parallel to the description of the parched land after the death of Aqhat. Later in the reign of David we read of a famine in the land which was attributed to Saul's slaying of the Gibeonites. Seven men of the family of Saul were slain (a kind of blood revenge), after which the famine was relieved (II Sam. 21:1-6).

With the thought that Aqhat had been killed while hunting, Danel sought to find the remains of his son in the vultures which were circling overhead. Traces of human flesh were found in a mother bird, and Danel gave them proper burial. A period of seven years of mourning was decreed. Meanwhile, Pughat determined to avenge the death of her brother. The story breaks off at this point due to the fact that the ending of the epic has not been discovered. We may presume that the missing portion of the story would tell how Yatpun was identified as the killer and slain. Under the influence of wine, Yatpun had boasted of his prowess in killing Aqhat. This is the last we read of him.

The motif of a famine lasting seven years is known from the Biblical story of Joseph of Egypt (Gen. 41:54). The epic use of the number seven is common to Biblical and other Near Eastern literature. The Israelites marched around Jericho seven times before the walls of the city fell (Josh. 6:3-4). In the Keret Epic, Pabil king of Udm was besieged for seven days. The vassals of Amenhotep III and IV state in the Amarna Letters that they bow seven times before their lord.

The description of a woman (Pughat) avenging the death of her brother is reminiscent of Jael, the woman who killed Sisera (Judg. 5:24-26). Brave women were as worthy of epic treatment as brave men. Blood revenge was an important factor in the early history of the Hebrews as of other Semetic peoples. It had particular significance in the absence of recognized government. The *go'el* had the responsibility for avenging the blood of a near kinsman. As late as the time of David we read that Joab used the *go'el* principle as an excuse for killing a potential rival, Abner, who had been Saul's general (II Sam. 3:27).

THE KERET EPIC

The epic of Keret tells the story of a righteous king who ruled a vast kingdom. Although outwardly prosperous, his achievements could not compensate for personal tragedy. Keret had

The Keret Text. The first of four texts in the cuneiform Ugaritic alphabet containing the legend of King Keret.

once chosen a wife for himself, but she ran away on the eve of the wedding. He was a king without children, and he grieved that there was none to succeed him on the throne. A series of catastrophies — death, pestilence, the sea, and battle — had removed each of Keret's brothers so that the king was left with no family ties whatever.

The great god El, seeing the tears of Keret, asked the king why he was weeping. Learning the cause of Keret's grief, El offered him larger estates, silver, and gold, but the king insisted that he had but one need — a family. Keret was satisfied with the measure of wealth that had been entrusted to him and the extent of the kingdom over which he ruled. His lack of sons was the one cause of grief.

The plight of the righteous Keret moved the heart of El. The great god instructed the king to offer appropriate sacrifices, bake sufficient bread for a campaign of six months (cf. Josh. 9:5) and call the people of his realm to arms. Only the widows, the sick, and the blind would be permitted to remain at home. Even the newly married, normally exempted from military service (cf. Deut. 24:5) would be required to go to war.

El instructed Keret to organize a campaign against Udm, the land of King Pabil. Keret was told that he would reach Pabil's capital after a march of six days. Pabil could be expected to offer Keret silver and gold on condition that he lift the siege imposed on the city. Keret, however, was told to reject the offer, demanding instead the hand of the princess Huriya "whose beauty is as the beauty of Anat, and whose grace is as the grace of Astarte" (Keret I, iii, 41-42).

Keret did not take the dream seriously at first, but he did offer the prescribed sacrifices and begin to muster his army. When all was in readiness the expedition set out for the land of Udm. On the third day they reached a shrine where Keret made a vow to Athirat of Tyre and Elat of Sidon. He pledged that upon receiving Huriya as bride he would present several times the value of the princess in silver and gold to the gods who had prospered his journey.

In due time Keret and his army reached Udm, thought by some scholars to be *Khirbet ed-Damiyeh* near the Sea of Galilee (cf. R. de Vaux, "Le Cadre geographique du poem de Keret," *Revue Biblique* XLVI [1937], pp. 362-372). As had been predicted, envoys from Pabil offered gifts to Keret on condition that he lift the siege, but Keret insisted that he would be satisfied with nothing less than the fair Huriya. When they realized that their situation was hopeless, the people of Udm bemoaned the loss of their princess and took her to the camp of Keret.

The god Baal interceded with El, asking the father of gods to bless the marriage of Keret. El promised that the wife of Keret would bear sons, one of whom, named Yassib, would be suckled by Athirat and the virgin Anat. This suggests that Keret's son would be adopted by the gods and become a demi-god in his own right. Six daughters were also promised to Keret, the youngest of whom would enjoy the rights of a firstborn child.

During the course of seven years Huriya bore sons and daughters to Keret, but the king forgot the vow he had made on the way to Udm. The goddess Athirat, after waiting seven years, decided to punish Keret by taking away his health. Her children, the other gods and goddesses, promised to do nothing to assist the king who had broken faith in the matter of his vow.

One day, as Keret's nobles were banqueting, Huriya brought news that the king was near death. Reactions in the royal family were varied. Yassib, Keret's firstborn was ready to take the throne for himself, but Elhu, the king's youngest son, gave evidence of genuine sorrow because of the sickness of the father he loved. Keret, weakened by his malady, urged Elhu to send for his sister Thitmanat ("the eighth") who was the youngest of the king's daughters. After making an offering to Baal, brother and sister entered the royal palace to visit their sick father.

We learn, however, that kindly El purposed to restore Keret to health. El asked the gods to send relief to Keret, but they had promised their mother Athirat that they would not assist the king who had forgotten his vow. Seven times El asked the gods to aid Keret but, caught in a conflict of loyalties, they continued to refuse. Finally El determined to help Keret without the aid of the gods. He sent the divine witch Sha'taqat ("she who removes sickness") to fly over towns and cities seeking a cure for Keret. She was evidently successful for, on her return to the palace, she announced that death had been vanquished. Sha'taqat touched Keret on the head and drove out his sickness. The faithful Huriya prepared food for her husband and, after three days, he was able to take his place on the throne again.

Yassib, Keret's firstborn, not knowing of the king's recovery came to the palace to urge his father to relinquish his throne. Keret, restored to full health, pronounced judgment on faithless Yassib whose sole concern was his own right of succession.

The epic breaks off at this point, but its conclusions may be reconstructed with little difficulty. The older sons and daughters of Keret had proved that they were only concerned with their own promotion, whereas the youngest, Elhu and Thitmanat, had given evidence of true love for their father. Doubtless Elhu succeeded to the throne after the king died — perhaps many years later — and Thitmanat received, as had been prophesied, the rights of the firstborn. These normally meant a double share in the inheritance.

Several of the motifs of the Keret Epic are familiar to the student of the Old Testament. The desire for a son was normal, and the greatest curse which could come upon a king was that which declared that his "seed" would be cut off (cf. I Kings 13:34).

The fact that God can speak to man in a dream is presupposed throughout the Old Testament, although revelation more frequently came through *Urim* (Num. 27:21), by means of a theophany (cf. Gen. 18:1) or through the ministry of a prophet (cf. Ezek. 3:17; 33:7). Even non-Israelites such as Pharaoh (Gen. 41:25-36) in the time of Joseph, and Nebuchadnezzar (Dan. 2:31-45; 4:4-27) in the time of Daniel received revelations in dreams.

The motif of the elder son becoming subservient to the younger appears in the Biblical account of Jacob and Esau. There we read of the supremacy of Jacob (Israel) over Esau (Edom) on the basis of (1) the divine purpose declared in prophecy (Gen. 25:23); (2) Esau's sale of his birthright (Gen. 25:31-32); and (3) Isaac's irrevocable blessing of Jacob (Gen. 27:27-29; cf. 27:39-49). Even though this blessing was secured by deceit, the sanctity of the spoken word made it binding.

THE BAAL EPIC

The story of Baal and Anat has been preserved on seven tablets from Ugarit, some of which are badly damaged. The outlines of the story can be followed with little difficulty, but the details and the exact sequence are often obscure.

At the beginning of the Baal Epic we are confronted with a problem. In order to function properly, Yam, the sea god, required an house. The kindly El, father of the gods, sent his messenger to Memphis, in Egypt, the abode of Ptah, where provision might be made to provide Yam with an house. International trade was commonplace at the time the Ugaritic epics were composed, and the Egyptian god of arts and crafts was identified with his Canaanite counterpart Kathir-and-Khasis. El's messenger was successful in his journey to Egypt, for the epic tells us that plans were soon under way to build Yam a suitable house.

When El announced plans for the house of Yam he also gave
him a new name, saying:

> The name of my son is Yaw god ...
> And he did proclaim the name of Yaw
> (Baal VI, iii, 14-15).

A new relationship warrants a new name. In Genesis 17:5 we
read how Abram, upon entering his covenant with Yahweh, became Abraham. After receiving his blessing at Peniel, Jacob received the name Israel (Gen. 32:28).

Consternation broke out among the gods when they learned
that Yam was to have his own house which would symbolize his
high status among the members of the pantheon. Athtar hastened
to El and urged the father of gods to prevent this exaltation of
Yam. Athtar was disappointed, however, for Shapash the sun
goddess told him that Yam would receive royal power. Athtar,
himself, might hope for power at a later time, but he could not
prevent Yam from occupying the house which would serve as his
palace.

Young Athtar had been unable to challenge the might of Yam,
but a more effective challenger came in the person of Baal, the
Canaanite god of fertility and storms. Accusing Yam of acting in
a high-handed manner, Baal called for the destruction of the
tyrant by Horon, god of pestilence, and the goddess Athtart-
name-of-Baal.

Angered at the insolence of Baal, Yam sent emissaries to the
assembly of the gods meeting at the Mount of El. There Yam de-
manded the surrender of Baal and his sympathizers. El, however,
did not take the matter seriously. He assured the messengers of
Yam that Baal would pay tribute to their master, and that they
were strong enough to overpower Baal if he should attempt to
give them trouble.

Subsequently a furious battle broke out between Baal and
Yam. A goddess, presumably Baal's sister Anat, discharged her
darts at Yam, but the god of the sea was unperturbed and the
goddess had to flee. The tide of battle turned, however, when
Kathir-and-Khasis promised victory to Baal and gave him two
magic maces with which to attack his rival. Baal used the two
weapons and was about to destroy Yam when Athtar rebuked
him for taking unfair advantage of a captive. Baal agreed to re-
lease Yam, but the contest had assured Baal the place of
supremacy.

A sumptuous feast was arranged to commemorate Baal's victory. While Baal ate and drank, a singer chanted songs in his
honor. Anat, however, closed the door of the palace and fell

ruthlessly upon Baal's enemies, wading through their blood up to her knees. Baal honored Anat's devotion but he urged her to lay aside her weapons. To demonstrate his power Baal created lightning to accompany the rain which he produced. Anat was asked to watch for the sounds of nature which precede the storm.

Baal had proved his power but, as yet, he had no house. Without an adequate palace he could not really rule. The faithful Anat took it upon herself to go to El and demand an house for Baal. There were the inevitable delays. Athirat was alarmed when Anat told her that the craftsman Hayin (another name for Kathir-and-Khasis) was at his forge ready to make furniture of silver and gold for Baal's house. Gifts from Baal and Anat quieted Athirat's fears and she decided to co-operate. Thereupon she ordered her fishermen to take a net and drag the sea for Yam who was again causing trouble.

Until Baal actually had an house of his own the other gods refused to show him proper respect. To bring the matter to a head, Athirat made a plea on behalf of Baal which El reluctantly accepted. He told Baal to assemble the necessary materials and workmen and proceed to build the house.

Cedars such as David and Solomon later used in their building operations (II Sam. 5:11; I Kings 5:8) were brought from Lebanon. Gold and silver was gathered from remote places and the craftsmen worked diligently on Baal's house. Within seven days it was completed and Baal was able to move in. Kathir-and-Khasis wanted to place a window in the house but Baal objected, fearing that his enemy Yam might be able to use it as a point of invasion.

When the house was completed, Baal's companions staged a great celebration but Baal was more concerned with his kingly responsibilities. He made his way to the seashore and smote Yam until there was no breath left in the monster. He then journeyed from city to city claiming each as part of his domain. In this way Baal was established with an house, and an empire to rule from it.

On his return Baal decided to allow Kathir-and-Khasis to insert windows in his house. His victories appear to have removed the fears which he had earlier entertained. From the newly made windows, Baal thundered, causing the earth to quake and his enemies to be terrified. Baal determined to destroy the archenemy Mot ("death") and thus secure uncontested rule over the universe. There is a logic in the rivalries expressed in the Baal Epic. The earth, Baal's domain, was threatened by encroachments from the sea (Yam), after which the blight of sterility (Mot) had to be removed.

As a challenge to Mot, Baal sent his messengers to the nether world with the announcement that he had acquired an house and claimed unchallenged right to the throne. Such a mission was dangerous, for the messengers were required to enter the realm of Mot who might devour them or destroy them with heat. Baal warned his messengers to make adequate preparation before approaching Mot.

The messengers were unharmed but Mot sent back to Baal a challenge to visit him in the nether world and partake of a feast there. Since those who eat of the food of the nether world can never return to the world above, Mot was actually seeking to lure Baal to his doom.

Although Baal would have preferred to provide his own feast for Mot, there was no way for Baal to bypass the challenge. Baal, accompanied by wind, cloud, and rain, with a retinue of attendants approached the gates of the nether world. The absence of Baal from his rightful domain would produce drought and famine. The fact that wind, clouds, and rain were missing from the earth would be accounted for by their presence with Baal in the nether world.

When it was learned that Baal had gone to the abode of Mot there was mourning among the gods. Young Athtar attempted to mount Baal's vacant throne, but his smallness of stature made it impossible. Athtar was the god of irrigation which can provide some moisture during the dry season but it cannot replace the rains which Baal alone provides. Athtar descended from Baal's throne but he was permitted to exercise a limited sovereignty.

Anat, however, remained faithful in her efforts to find her missing brother. During the absence of Baal the sun was unbearably hot, there was no rain, and the land was parched. Anat who was goddess of war as well as love, sought satisfaction from Mot, but he would not restore her brother. In anger Anat took the god of death, cut up his body, and threw the pieces to the birds who ate them.

In a dream El learned that Baal was alive in the nether world. Since the sun descends to the nether world each night, the sun goddess was asked to find him and bring him back to the world of mankind on his next circuit. This was accomplished and the faithful Anat soon proclaimed the good news that Baal would revisit the earth accompanied by bountiful showers which would rain on the parched ground. It was as though life had defeated death!

The opening motif of the Baal Epic — the need to provide an house for a god who claims the right of rule — has a faint echo in Scripture. G. R. Driver notes that "Solomon's palace visibly proved his right to a disputed throne" (*Canaanite Myths and Legends*, p. 16). David, after capturing Jerusalem from the Jebusites, built an house for himself and proposed to build one for his God: "See now, I dwell in a house of cedar, but the ark of God dwells in a tent" (II Sam. 7:22). Although Yahweh's power was in no sense abridged before the Temple was built, it was deemed appropriate that the reigning king and the God whom he served should each have a suitable house. The kingship of Yahweh is a recurring theme in the Old Testament. The Tabernacle was his palace, and the Holy of Holies served as his throne room (Exod. 25:22; Num. 7:89; Ps. 80:1). The concept of theocracy during the period of the Judges gave emphasis to the immediate rule of God. The Hebrew language uses the same word to describe the palace of the king or the Temple of God. It is derived from the Sumerian *E GAL*, literally "big house" and distinguished the abodes of gods and kings from the humbler dwellings of lesser beings.

VIII

THE UGARITIC TEXTS AND THE BIBLE

Whatever adds to our knowledge of the ancient Near East adds to our knowledge of the Bible because of the geographical and historical relations which existed between Israel and her neighbors. This is particularly true of Ugarit due to the similarity of language between Israel and Ugarit and the geographical proximity of the peoples.

HISTORICAL BACKGROUNDS

After her entrance into Canaan, Israel was constantly tempted to adopt the idolatrous practices of the earlier inhabitants of the land. The Moabites introduced Israel to the licentious Baal worship in the orgy of Baal-peor (Num. 25:1-9) and idolatry was rampant in Israel by the time of the Judges (Judg. 2:11-23). The Ugaritic texts illustrate the place which Baal held in the Canaanite religion of patriarchal times. As a fertility god, it was Baal to whom the Canaanites looked for food and fecunity among animals and men. The Israelites entered Canaan from the wilderness and were unaccustomed to agricultural techniques. Canaanites taught them not only the best methods of sowing and reaping, but also the worship of Baal and the other gods who challenged the Lordship of Yahweh over his covenant people.

LEGAL TERMINOLOGY

Many of the sacrifices mentioned in the Ugaritic texts have names which are identical to those described in the book of Leviticus. Ugaritic texts speak of the Burnt Offering, the Whole Burnt Offering, the Trespass Offering, the Offering for Expiation of the Soul; the Wave Offering, the Tribute Offering, the First Fruits Offering, the Peace Offering, and the New Moon Offering. The term "offering without blemish" also appears in the Ugaritic literature.

57

Although Moses is rightly regarded as the Israelite lawgiver, the Old Testament does not imply that the sacrificial system associated with his name had its beginnings at Sinai. Sacrifices are mentioned as early as the time of Cain and Abel (Gen. 4:3-5), and Noah is said to have made Burnt Offerings after leaving the ark (Gen. 8:20). Abraham and his immediate descendants regularly offered sacrifices (Gen. 22:13; 26:25; 33:20). The sacrificial system of Israel was codified as a part of the Mosaic law, but its origins are much earlier. The Ugaritic documents attest to the antiquity of such sacrifices as we meet on the pages of the Old Testament.

Elements which Israelites and Canaanites held in common may be traced to the common traditions possessed by the two peoples concerning worship. The New Testament insists that there was a genuine revelation of God to the pre-Abrahamic peoples which was never completely forgotten (Rom. 1:21-32).

Having noted similarities between the sacrificial language of Ugarit and the Bible, it is important to observe the differences as well. The sacrifices of Ugarit were directed to Baal and a host of other gods whose worship was abhorrent to the prophets of Israel. Cultic prostitution, a normal element in Canaanite religion, was strictly forbidden in Israel.

The Ugaritic epic entitled, "The Birth of the Beautiful and Gracious Gods" describes the rite of seething a kid in its mother's milk in order to produce rain for the parched soil of Canaan. This rite was specifically forbidden in Israelite law (Exod. 23:1; 34:26). Observant Jews interpret this command in such a way that they do not eat dairy and meat products at the same meal. Originally it appears to have been a polemic against Canaanite Baal worship which was a constant threat to Israel's loyalty to Yahweh.

VOCABULARY

Hebrew is written in a consonantal alphabet. The system of indicating vowels now used in printed Hebrew Bibles was devised centuries after the Scriptures were first written. These vowel points are of value in showing the traditional pronunciation of the Hebrew Scriptures, but they have no inherent authority. The original consonantal text might be illustrated by the English letters *bd*. Standing alone the combination of two consonants might represent the words bad, bed, bid, bide, bud, and even such combinations as abide, abode. It would be necessary to determine from the context how the letters *bd* should be pronounced in a given sentence. The Hebrew root system was such that most words with identical consonants had related meanings, so the illustration is not in all respects accurate. Nevertheless there are debatable readings, and scholars are much more willing to suggest changes in the vowels than in the consonantal text of the Hebrew Bible.

The Hebrew root *kbd* suggests the idea of heaviness. It is used of the liver, a heavy organ, and — in a very different sense — it conveys the idea of glory. The King James Version of Psalm 16:9a reads:

> Therefore my heart is glad
> And my glory rejoiceth.

In Ugarit, however, we meet the lines,

> El laughs in his heart
> And is convulsed with mirth in his liver.

The liver was thought to be the seat of the emotions, and we frequently meet it in parallel structure with "heart." The original thought of Psalm 16:9a would seem to be:

> Therefore my heart is glad
> And my liver rejoices.

The English language uses "heart" in a metaphorical sense, designating the inner man and his affections — particularly love. "Liver," however, never acquired such a use. The Revised Standard Version translated *kbd* by "soul" in this passage:

> Therefore my heart is glad
> And my soul rejoices.

Although this is not strictly-speaking literal, it does indicate the concept of the inner man. "Heart" and "soul" are parallel ideas in English, whereas, except in physiology, "heart" and "liver" are not. In this instance the Ugaritic text suggests that we might reject the translation "my glory" and substitute "my soul" which is closer to the original idea.

The same word appears in Genesis 49:6 where Jacob mentions the perfidy of Simeon and Levi. In the light of Ugaritic usage we could read literally:

> Into their society, come not my soul,
> In their assembly, rejoice not my liver!

The Greek word for liver was actually used in the Greek Septuagint. The King James translators rendered it:

> O my soul, come not thou into their secret,
> Unto their assembly, mine honor, be not thou united.

As in Psalm 16:9a, the King James Version renders *kbd* in the sense of "honor" or "glory," with no hint of the Semitic concept of *kbd*, "liver." Here the Revised Standard Version used the word "spirit," doubtless because it seemed an appropriate parallel to "soul":

O my soul, come not into their council,
O my spirit, be not joined to their company.

The translator is faced with the necessity of rendering concepts as well as words into the understandable idiom of the language in which he wishes the Scriptures to be read. Here the Ugaritic has been of help in clearing up a mistranslation, but it has been difficult to convey the exact sense of the original into meaningful English.

The discovery of a new corpus of literature in a Semitic language closely akin to Biblical Hebrew has made it possible to study Biblical words in a wider context than was previously known. The Hebrew word *bamôt* often appears in the Old Testament in the sense of "high places," the infamous s,ites of idolatrous worship denounced by the prophets of Israel (cf. Ezek. 16:24, 25, 31). The corresponding word appears in Ugaritic with the primary sense of the back of a person or animal. It is in this sense that Cyrus H. Gordon suggests that we translate Deuteronomy 33:29:

Thy enemies shall be discomfited before thee,
Thou shalt treat upon their backs *(bamôt)*.
— *Ugritic Manual*, Glossary, word 332

This translation accords with the artistic portrayals from the ancient Near East which depict a conqueror with his foot upon the back of his victim. The rendering "backs" rather than "high places" is more meaningful in Deuteronomy 33:29.

M. J. Dahood has suggested a revision of Ecclesiastes 3:11b in the light of Ugaritic usage. Traditionally the passage is rendered:

He has put eternity into man's mind, yet so that he cannot find out what God has done from the beginning to the end.

Dahood notes that the Ugaritic equivalent of '*ôlam*, "age, eternity," is '*glm* which means "to grow dark." Suggesting that Ecclesiastes was influenced by this usage, he translates the passage:

Yea he set darkness in their hearts so that man discovers not the work which God has done.

The Ugaritic evidence also leads Dahood to suggest a different reading for Ecclesiastes 12:6b. The King James Version reads:

. . . or the pitcher be broken at the fountain
or the wheel broken at the cistern.

The word rendered "wheel" appears as "bowl" in Ugaritic, and this forms a better parallel to pitcher, or jar. The passage would then read

. . . and the jar is broken at the spring
and the pot is shattered at the well-head.

The King James Version reads in Genesis 1:2

... and the Spirit of God moved upon the face of the waters. The picture conveyed by the word translated "moved" has puzzled translators for some years. The English Revised Version (1885) expanded "moved" into "was brooding over." This sense has now been found in Ugarit where the corresponding root (*rhp*) is used to describe a bird flying or soaring over a place.

When King Uzziah was stricken with leprosy he was placed in "a several house" according to the traditional reading of II Kings 15:5 and II Chronicles 26:21. The meaning of the term was not clear. It was translated "a separate house" in the American Standard and Revised Standard Versions. Now the corresponding term is found in the Ugaritic texts to describe the place to which Al ;yan Baal descended before proceeding to the nether world. This leads to the thought that Uzziah was confined to a cave or cellar, perhaps even the palace basement.

Textual Studies

David's lament over Saul and Jonathan following their death on Mount Gilboa contains the lines:

> Ye mountains of Gilboa,
> let there be no dew nor rain upon you,
> neither fields of offerings (II Sam. 1:21).

Biblical scholars have been puzzled over the expression "fields of offering," but H. L. Ginsberg, has proposed a solution which has been widely accepted. In the Aqhat Epic we read a curse which is similar to that which David uttered:

> Seven years may Baal fail
> Even eight, the rider of the clouds;
> Nor dew, nor rain, nor upsurging of the deep,
> Nor sweetness of the voice of Baal.

The Hebrew word for "fields" is similar to the Ugaritic word for "upsurging" and the Hebrew "offering" is similar to the Ugaritic "deep." Ginsberg suggests, on the basis of this parallel, that David prayed:

> Ye mountains of Gilboa,
> let there be no dew nor rain upon you,
> neither upsurging of the deep.
> — "A Ugaritic Parallel to 2 Samuel 1:21,"
> JBL, LVII (1938), pp. 209-13.

The Revised Standard Version has accepted this interpretation. The "upsurgings of the deep" were the mountain springs, as we know from the Ugaritic texts. Dew, rain, and mountain springs were the three sources of moisture in Syria and Palestine. David prayed that there would be no dew, rain, nor moun-

tain springs to irrigate Mount Gilboa. The barren mount would
thus be seen as mourning for Saul and Jonathan.

The people of Ugarit are known to have used a white glaze
which is termed *spsg* in the tablets. The word appears in Proverbs 26:23 although it was not recognized by the ancient scribes
who made two words out of it. In the light of Ugaritic usage the
verse should doubtless be read:

> Burning lips and a wicked heart are like white glaze covered over
> a pot.

LITERARY ALLUSIONS

The existence of a large body of Canaanite literature makes
it possible for us to compare figures of speech and literary
modes of expression as they existed in Israel and in Ugarit. Just
as we draw upon classical mythology for many of our Western
speech patterns, so the Israelites and their neighbors draw upon
a stock of similes and metaphors which was common to the
ancient Semitic peoples.

Although Baal was predominantly a fertility god, and Israel
officially rejected the entire Baal cult, many things which were
said by the Canaanites about Baal could also be said by the
Israelites about Yahweh. Baal was the Canaanite fertility god,
but the Israelites insisted that it was Yahweh who "maketh hinds
to calve" (Ps. 29:9). The God of Israel was looked upon as
author of the blessings of heaven (rain); of the deep (springs);
and of breast and womb (Gen. 49:25; Deut. 33:13).

The Ugaritic texts frequently describe Baal as "rider of the
clouds," for it was he who produced rain. The same expression
is used in Scripture of Yahweh (Ps. 68:4, 33; Deut. 33:26;
Isa. 19:1), for the God of the Bible was regarded as sovereign
over all the forces of nature. Thunder was His voice (cf.
Ps. 29:3) and he sent forth arrows in the form of lightning
(Ps. 18:13-14).

When the author of the Biblical flood story wanted to describe the torrents of rain which fell upon the earth he used
the poetic expression, "The windows of heaven were opened"
(Gen. 7:11). The Baal Epic tells how the god Baal was at first
reluctant to have windows in his house lest they provide a means
of access for his enemy. When, however, he permitted windows
to be placed in his temple in the skies:

> Baal opened a window in the mansion,
> a lattice in the midst of the palace,
> he opened a skylight (in the roof).
> Baal uttered his holy voice,

> Baal repeated the issue of his lips,
> (even) his holy voice; the earth quaked
> ......the rocks were dismayed
> ..were perturbed
> east (and) west the high places of the earth
> rocked   (Baal II, vi, 25-35).

Thunder is described as the voice of Baal, and from the open windows of Baal's temple he thundered his storms upon the world of men.

The mythological figure Lotan was an enemy of the god Baal. He appears in the Bible as Leviathan. The Baal epic says:

> When thou smotest Leviathan the slippery serpent (and) madest
> an end of the wriggling serpent, the tyrant with seven heads...
> (*Baal I.* i.* 1-3).

The words are reminiscent of Isaiah 27:1

> In that day the Lord [i.e. Yahweh] with his great and strong sword
> will punish Leviathan, the twisting serpent, and he will slay the
> dragon that is in the sea.

The Biblical Leviathan, like Ugaritic Lotan, had a multiplicity of heads:

> Thou didst crush the heads of leviathan (Ps. 74:14).

It should be noted, however, that Biblical Leviathan, unlike his Ugaritic counterpart, was not a god. Leviathan was a rebellious creature of Yahweh. He represents the forces of evil which come under divine judgment. The high ethical monotheism of the Israelites finds no parallel in the ancient Near East, and no literature is truly comparable with the Biblical records.

HISTORICAL ALLUSIONS

When King Hezekiah was sick with a boil, the prophet Isaiah directed that a cake or lump of figs be placed on the boil (II Kings 20:7; Isa. 38:21). We learn from one of the veterinary treatises from Ugarit that lumps of figs were used as poultices for horses. The medicinal use of figs appears to have had a long history.

The prophet Ezekiel mentioned three godly men who were the epitome of righteousness: Noah, Daniel, and Job (Ezek. 14:14-20). Both Noah and Job were men of the ancient past at the time of Ezekiel's prophecy, but the young Daniel was a contemporary of Ezekiel. It has long seemed unusual to link Daniel with the worthies of the distant past, but the Ugaritic texts give us reason to think that Ezekiel was referring to an earlier Daniel, or Danel. Danel of the Ugaritic texts was a righteous king who:

> ...judged the cause of the widow and he tried the case of the
> orphan   (Aqhat II. v. 6-7).

In addressing the "prince of Tyre" (Ezek. 28:2-3) the prophet
said scornfully, "Behold! You are indeed wiser than Daniel, no
secret is hidden from you." Tyre, like Ugarit, was in the ancient
land of Phoenicia. Its king might be expected to have known of
the ancient Danel, famed for wisdom and justice.

King David purchased the threshingfloor of a man designated
as "Araunah the Jebusite" (II Sam. 24:18). The Ugaritic texts
contain a word *iwr*, meaning "lord." It forms a part of several
personal names and appears in the name *iwrn*.

The word Araunah appears to be a Hebrew spelling of the
Ugaritic *iwrn*, a word of Hurrian origin. It means "the lord" and
was the title of a chief in Jebusite Jerusalem. In the Authorized
Version of II Samuel 24:23:

> All these things did Araunah *as* a king unto the king . . . .

the word "as" was supplied by the translators. Actually the
word "a king" (lit. "the king") is a Hebrew translation of the
word Araunah. The passage might thus be read:

> All these things did Araunah [i.e., the king] give unto the king
> [i.e., David].

POETIC STRUCTURE

Semitic poetry differs from that of modern western languages
in that the Semites did not consider rhyme or meter essential to
poetic expression. Instead they used the phenomena of parallelism. There was no mechanical regularity about parallelistic structure, but in general the poetic lines expressed synonymous or an-
tithetic thoughts. An instance of synonymous parallelism occurs
in Isaiah 1:2:

> Hear, O heavens,
> and give ear, O earth.

In this passage the words "hear" and "give ear" are synonymous.
Although "heavens" and "earth" are opposites, no stress is placed
upon the differences. Actually all of the universe is called upon
to hear the word of Yahweh.

Such lines occur in the Ugaritic literature, as they do among
the writings of all the ancient Semitic peoples. In Ugarit we
read:

> The heavens rain oil,
> The wadies run with honey.

Two sources of water are before the writer: the heavens from
which rain falls upon the land, and the wadies which bring
moisture to the land around them during the rainy seasons. Oil
and honey, representative of prosperity in the land, are seen as
the result of the activity of the heavens and the wadies.

A longer bit of poetry from Ugarit, addressed to Baal, reads:

Lo thine enemies, O Baal,
Lo thine enemies wilt thou smite,
Lo thou wilt cut off thine adversary
Thou wilt win thine everlasting kingdom,
Thy dominion of generation and generation.

The style of these lines reminds us of Psalm 92:9:

For lo thine enemies O Lord
For lo thine enemies shall perish
All evildoers shall be scattered.

The latter lines of the Ugaritic passage have much in common with Psalm 145:13:

Thy kingdom is an everlasting kingdom
And thy dominion endures throughout all generations.

In some instances Ugaritic poetry not only is similar in structure to that of the Old Testament but it uses the same language. When Kathir-and-Khasis, the Canaanite god of arts and crafts, agreed to build a temple for Baal:

(They hasted) to build his mansion,
(They hasted) to construct his palace.
They went to Lebanon and its trees
to Siryon (and) its choicest cedars...
(Baal II. vi. 16-19).

Lebanon was the source of wood for Solomon's Temple (I Kings 5:6) as it was for building operations both in Egypt and Mesopotamia in ancient times. Sirion was the Phoenician name for Hermon (Deut. 3:9, where the Phoenicians are termed Sidonians from their city of Sidon) and it is mentioned with Lebanon in Psalm 29:6.

A common poetical phenomenon of Scripture is the climactic use of numbers. The writer states a number, and then follows it with the next larger number to give emphasis to his statement. The prophet Amos used a series of such, beginning with:

For three transgressions of Tyre, and for four, I will
not turn away the punishment thereof
(Amos 1:9, cf. 1:11, 13; 2:1, 4, 6).

A similar pattern is used in Proverbs:

There be three things which are too wonderful for me;
yea, four which I know not...(Prov. 30:18).

The Baal Epic uses numerical climax to describe the attitude of the fertility god to sacrifice:

Lo! (there are) two sacrifices (which) Baal, three
(which) the rider of the clouds does hate: a sacrifice
of shame and a sacrifice
of meanness and a sacrifice of the lewdness
of handmaids   (Baal II, iii, 16-20).

When Anat approached the venerable El to plead for her brother Baal we read:

The bull El her father lifted up his voice
from the seven chambers, (from) the eight (openings)
of the closed room(?)   (Baal V, v, 11).

The climatic use of numbers is exhibited in the description of
Baal's journey which he made to claim the domains which were
rightly his after he was furnished with a temple:

... he did seize six and sixty
cities, seventy-seven towns,
he became lord of (eight and) eighty, lord
of nine and ninety   (Baal II, vii, 9-12).

We should not conclude that the Israelites directly borrowed
their literary forms from Ugarit. Both peoples drew upon a literary and cultural inheritance which was common to the western
Semites and, in a measure, to all Near Eastern peoples. The
ancient inhabitants of the Fertile Crescent were highly mobile.
Ugarit was not only linked to the Fertile Crescent — reaching
southward to Egypt and eastward to the lands of the Tigris-
Euphrates basin — but also enjoyed the cultural advantage of
trade with the Mediterranean islands, particularly Cyprus, and
with the Hittite Empire.

BIBLIOGRAPHY

Translation of Ugaritic Texts

Aisleitner, J., Die Mythologischen und Kultischen Texte aus Ras Shamra. Budapest: Akademiai Kidao, 1959.
Driver, G. R., Canaanite Myths and Legends, Edinburgh: T. & T. Clark, 1956.
Gaster, Theodor, The Oldest Stories in the World. New York: Viking Press, 1952.
Ginsberg, H. L., "Ugaritic Myths and Legends," Ancient Near Eastern Texts, ed. J. B. Pritchard. Princeton: Princeton University Press, 1953.
Gordon, Cyrus H., Ugaritic Literature. Rome: Pontifical Biblical Institute, 1949.

Studies in the Ugaritic Texts

Baumgartner, W., "Ras Schamra und das Alte Testament," Theologische Rundschau, XII (1940), 163-188.
Cassuto, U., The Goddess Anath. Jerusalem: The Bialik Institute, 1958.
Cazelles, H., "Ras Schemra und der Pentateuch," Theologische Quartelschrift, CXXXVIII (1958), 26-39.
DeLanghe, R., Le Textes de Ras Shamra-Ugarit et leurs Rapports avec le Milieu de l'Ancien Testament. Paris: Desclee de Brouwer, 1943.
———, "Myth, Ritual, and Kingship in the Ras Shamra Tablets," Myth, Ritual, and Kingship, ed. S. H. Hooke. Oxford: Clarendon Press, 1958.
Dussaud, R., Les decouvertes de Ras Shamra et l'Ancien Testament, Second Edition.
Gaster, Theodor, "The Religion of the Canaanites," Forgotten Religions, ed. V. Ferm. New York: Philosophical Library, 1950.

67

———,*Thespis.* New York: Henry Schumann, 1950.

Gordon, Cyrus H., "Ugaritic as Link between Greek and Hebrew Literature," *"Rivista degli Studi Orientali,* XXIX 1954), 161-169.

———, *Ugaritic Manual,* Rome: Pontifical Biblical Institute, 1955.

Gray, John, "Canaanite Kingship in Theory and Practice," *Vetus Testamentum* II (1952), 193-220.

———, "Canaanite Mythology and Hebrew Tradition," *Transactions of the Glasgow University Oriental Society,* XIV (1953), 47-57.

———, "Cultic Affinities between Israel and Ras Shamra," *Zeitschrift fur die alttestamentliche Wissenschaft,* LXII (1949). 207-220.

———, "The Desert God Aṭtr in the Literature and Religion of Canaan," *Journal of Near Eastern Studies,* VIII (1949), 72-83.

———, "Feudalism in Ugarit and Early Israel," *Zeitschrift fur die alttestamentliche Wissenschaft,* XLIV (1952), 49-55.

———, *The Krt Text in the Literature of Ras Shamra.* Leiden: E. J. Brill, 1955.

———, *The Legacy of Canaan.* Leiden: E. J. Brill, 1957.

Jack, J. W., *The Ras Shamra Tablets; Their Bearing on the Old Testament.* Edinburgh: T. & T. Clark, 1935.

Jacob, Edmond, *Ras Shamra et L'Ancien Testament.* Neuchatel: Editions Delachaux et Niestle, 1960.

Kaiser, O., *Die mythische Bedeutung des Meeres in Agypten, Ugarit, und Israel.* Berlin: Topelmann, 1959.

Kapelrud, Arvid S., *Baal in the Ras Shamra Texts.* Copenhagen: G. E. C. Gadd, 1952.

Montgomery, J. A., "Notes on the Mythological Epic Texts of Ras Shamra," *Journal of the American Oriental Society,* LIII (1933), 97-123.

———, "Additional Notes on the Ras Shamra Texts," *Journal of the American Oriental Society,* LIII (1933), 283-284.

———, "Ras Shamra Notes II," *Journal of the American Oriental Society,* LIV (1934), 60-66.

———, "Ras Shamra Notes III," *Journal of the American Oriental Society,* LV (1935), 89-94.

———, "Ras Shamra Notes IV: The Conflict of Baal and the Waters," *Journal of the American Oriental Society,* LV (1935), 268-277.

———, "Ras Shamra Notes V," *Journal of the American Oriental Society,* LVI (1936), 226-231.

――, "Ras Shamra Notes VI: the Danel Text," *Journal of the American Oriental Society*, LVI (1936), 440-445.

――, "The New Sources of Knowledge," *Record and Revelation*, ed. H. Wheeler Robinson. Oxford: Clarendon Press, 1938.

Obermann, Julian, "How Baal Destroyed a Rival," *Journal of the American Oriental Society*, LXVII (1948), 195-208.

――, *Ugaritic Mythology*. New Haven: Yale University Press, 1948.

O'Callaghan, Roger T., "Echoes of Canaanite Literature in the Psalms," *Vetus Testamentum*, IV (1954), 164-176.

Otten, H., "Ein Kanaanaischer Mythus aus Bogazkoy," *Mitteilungen des Instituts fur Orientforschung*, I (1953), 125-130.

Pope, Marvin H., *El in the Ugaritic Texts*. Leiden: E. J. Brill, 1055.

Richardson, H. Neil, "Ugaritic Parallels to the Old Testament," Unpublished doctoral dissertation, Boston University School of Theology, 1957.

Schaeffer, Claude F. A., *The Cuneiform Texts of Ras Shamra-Ugarit*. The Schweich Lectures, 1936. London: British Academy (Oxford), 1939.

De Vaux, R., "Le cadre geographique du poeme de Keret," *Revue Biblique* XLVI (1937), 362-372.

――, "Les textes de Ras Shamra et l'Ancien Testament," *Revue Biblique* XLVI (1937), 362-372.

Virolleaud, C. *Legendes de Babylone et de Canaan*. Paris: A. Maisonneuve, 1949.

――, *La Legende de Keret, roi des Sidoniens* (Mission de Ras Shamra, II). Paris: Paul Geuthner, 1936.

Worden, T., "The Literary Influence of the Ugaritic Fertility Myth on the Old Testament," *Vetus Testamentum*, III (1953), 273-298.

Archaeological Backgrounds

Albright, W. F., *Archaeology and the Religion of Israel*. Baltimore: Johns Hopkins Press, 1953.

――, *From the Stone Age to Christianity*. Baltimore: Johns Hopkins Press, 1940.

Breasted, James H., *Ancient Records of Egypt*. Chicago: University of Chicago Press, 1907.

Burrows, Millar, *What Mean These Stones?* New Haven: Yale University Press, 1941.

Cook, Stanley A., *The Religion of Ancient Palestine in the Light of Archaeology.* The Schweich Lectures, 1925. London: British Academy (Oxford), 1930.

Cumont, Franz, *The Oriental Religions in Roman Paganism* New York: Dover Publications, reprint (original edition, 1911).

Eissfeldt, Otto, "El and Yahweh," *Journal of Semitic Studies,* I (1956), 25-37.

Frazer, James, *The Golden Bough,* ed. Theodor Gaster. New York: Criterion Books, 1959.

Gordon, Cyrus H., *The World of the Old Testament.* Garden City, N.Y.: Doubleday and Company, 1958.

Guirand, F., "Assyro-Babylonian Mythology," *Larousse Encyclopedia of Mythology.* New York: Promethius Press, 1959, 49-72.

Kaufmann, Yehezkel, "The Biblical Age," *Great Ages and Ideas of the Jewish People,* ed. Leo W. Schwarz. New York: Random House, 1956, 3-92.

Knudtzon, J. A., *Die El-Amarna Tafeln.* Leipzig: J. C. Hinrichs'sche Buchhandlung, 1908-15.

INDEX

71